# ART

## FOR CHILDREN

### A STEP-BY-STEP GUIDE FOR THE YOUNG ARTIST

# ART
## FOR CHILDREN

A STEP-BY-STEP GUIDE FOR
THE YOUNG ARTIST

CHARTWELL
BOOKS, INC.

# A QUARTO BOOK

ISBN: 0-7858-0708-X

This book was designed and produced by
Quarto Children's Books Limited
The Fitzpatrick Building
188-194 York Way
London N7 9QP

Manufactured by Bright Arts (Pte) Ltd, Singapore
Printed by Star Standard Industries (Pte) Ltd, Singapore

Published by Chartwell Books Inc
A Division of Book Sales Inc
114 Northfield Avenue
Edison, New Jersey 08837

# CONTENTS

## Creative Crafts

# Getting started

IN THIS BOOK THERE ARE LOTS OF DIFFERENT crafts for you to try. Each section shows projects which are simple enough for beginners, and there are lots of suggestions for other ideas to experiment with. The projects have all been designed so that you can get good results quickly and cheaply.

▲ *A papier mache bowl makes a great gift for a special someone!*

### SUCCESSFUL CRAFTS

Before you choose which craft idea to make, think about who it is for and how it will be used.

If you are making something as a present for someone, think about the kind of taste they have: for instance, what style of clothes they wear and what ornaments they have in their home. If you follow their taste when you make something for them, your present is more likely to be a success.

If you are making something for yourself, use your favorite colors. You could even work your name or references to your hobbies into the design.

If you are making something to display in a particular room, think what color the room is, and then match or contrast the colors of the craft item you intend to make. You could adapt the design according to the activity in a particular room; for instance, you could use images of different foods for a kitchen object, and images of fish, boats, and mermaids for a bathroom object.

▲ *This snake is made by a method of fabric painting known as batik.*

ne

cotton reels

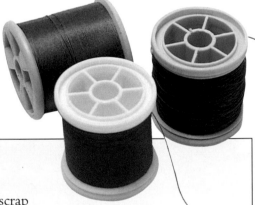

---

## CRAFT KIT

It's a good idea to start gathering together a basic craft kit which will be useful whichever project you try. You will need to buy some of the items, but you can collect the others over time.

• Buy a pencil, water-washable glue, sticky tape, scissors, water-washable paints, a selection of paintbrushes, and a set of crayons. A sketchpad would be useful, too.
• For some of the crafts in this book you also need a small sewing kit, including pins, a needle, and some thread.

• Collect scrap paper and card, clean empty plastic pots and cartons, scrap fabric, wool, and catalogues.
• To store your craft kit, get a large empty cardboard box (you could find one in a supermarket). Decorate the box with paint or cut-out paper shapes.
• Buy a few special items for some crafts, such as fabric paints or cold-water dye.
• Before you start a craft, make sure you read the instructions for the product you buy.

## CHOOSING A CRAFT

*▲ Designing your own wrapping paper makes a present really special.*

When you choose a craft to try, bear in mind how much time you have and how much money you want to spend to get the equipment and materials you need. For instance, if you want to complete a craft in a few hours, don't choose papier mache, which takes a few days to complete. If you don't want to buy any extra materials, try a craft such as collage, using items you already have around the house.

Don't worry if you don't get the exact results shown in the book. Use the photographs of objects as guides to help you create your own original pieces.

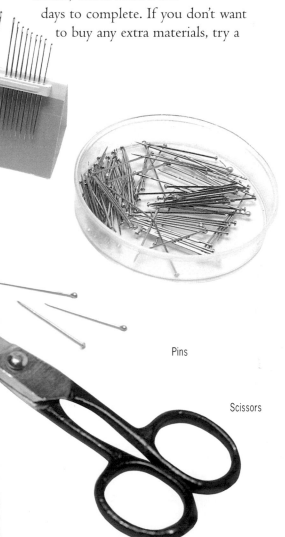

Pins

Scissors

Poster paints and paintbrush

# Craft planning

**B**EFORE YOU START A CRAFT IT IS important to plan your work carefully. Make rough sketches and color them in with crayons or felt-tip pens, so you have some idea of what the finished design will be.

Colored paper

### DESIGN RESEARCH

You may find that there is something special that you want to draw or paint. For instance, you may want to make a design in the shape of an animal. In that case, go to the library and find a book that shows you the shape and colors you need. You could also put real objects in front of you, such as leaves and flowers, and copy what you see.

Many of the crafts in this book are traditional. Once you get interested in a particular method, go to the library and find books on craft techniques and design in history. Look out for inspiration in museums and art galleries, too.

### DESIGNING IDEAS

Gather together pencils, crayons, an eraser, a ruler, some plain scrap paper or a sketchpad, and some tracing paper.

Draw three or four simple outlines of the object you want to make and then use crayons to get different effects. Don't worry about making your design look realistic. Instead, concentrate on the mix of colors you will use and the shapes you want to show. It is often best to keep the design simple. That way, the effect you want will be easier to achieve.

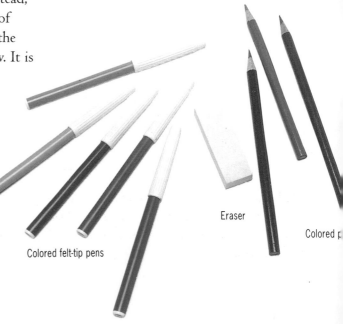

Colored felt-tip pens

Eraser

Colored p

Stencil paper

Tracing paper

## SKETCHING AND TRACING

When you are planning your work it may help if you look at references to copy or to inspire new ideas of your own. For instance, if you are fabric-painting a T-shirt you may want to find a photo or a magazine picture to copy. Trace the outline of the picture. Then cut out the traced shape and draw round it onto the fabric or the paper you are using for your craft.

## ENLARGING A DESIGN

You may find a reference picture that you want to enlarge to fit your craft object. Here's how:

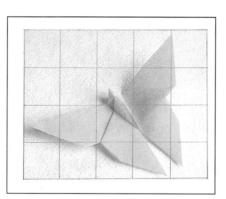

*I First, draw a square grid over the picture. Use a ruler and pencil to do this, dividing it up into equal squares. If you don't want to draw directly onto the reference, tape tracing paper over it and draw your grid onto this.*

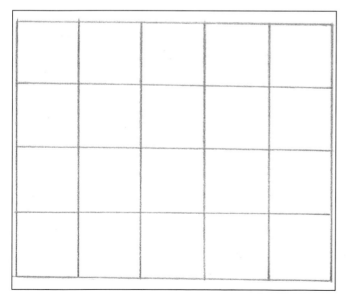

*2 Decide roughly how big you want the picture to be (for instance, twice or three times as big as the original). Then, draw a larger grid on paper with the same number of squares, but that much bigger.*

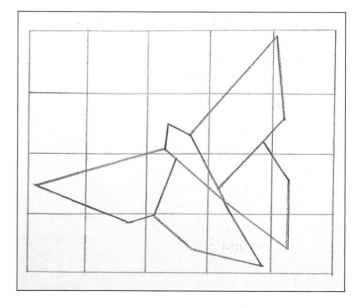

*3 Using the first, smaller grid as a guide, copy the picture onto the larger grid you have made. Notice which parts of the picture fit into which square. The squares in the grid shown above are twice the size of the squares in the smaller grid.*

# Paper flowers

Paper and thin card can be cut and folded to make all kinds of clever-looking objects! Either use pre-colored paper, or paint onto it before or after you have made a model. Keep a collection of paper scraps in an envelope or folder so that you always have pieces to use. Start by practicing the basic techniques shown below.

## SCORING CARD

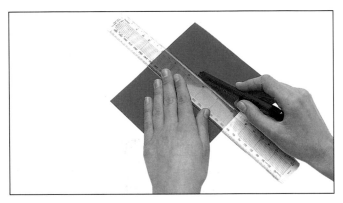

1 *To make a neat fold in thin card, it is best to "score" the foldline first by laying a ruler along the line and "drawing" along the ruler edge with the blunt edge of a pair of scissors.*

2 *Fold the foldline, bending the card the opposite way to the scored line. It will fold with a neat, sharp edge.*

## PAPER FLOWERS

Use paper folding to make these pretty flowers. They will last much longer than the real thing, so they make an ideal present.

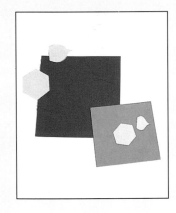

1 *Cut out a six-sided template from one piece of card and a petal shape from another piece. Place the first template in the center of a piece of colored paper and draw round it. Place the petal template against each side in turn, tracing round it each time to make a flower shape with equal-sized petals.*

2 *Make a smaller flower shape in the same way, using different-colored paper. Then, cut both flower shapes and glue the smaller shape onto the center of the larger one.*

◀ *To make an unusual table decoration, try floating your favorite selection of paper flowers in a glass bowl filled with colored water.*

Put some paint or ink in the water to color it.

**3** *Cut out a circle of paper for the center of the flower. Snip into the edge all the way around and bend the frayed edge upwards. Stick this onto the center of the flower with glue. Bend the petals upward to make the flower look more realistic.*

**4** *You can make lots of flowers in this way, with different size and color petals and center. If you like, cut some leaves and glue them to the flower shapes. Make them long and spiky, or rounded and feathery.*

For stems use long, thin tubes of green card.

Cut out leaves and glue them to the inside top of the vase.

▲ *This paper vase is ideal for displaying your flowers. Make it by gluing strips of colored card around a toilet-roll tube. Then cut flaps at the top, fold and glue to the back of the flowers.*

# Paper puppets

MAKE A MOUSE AND SOME walking finger puppets decorated with folded and curled paper. Then make a little stage for them to perform on. They make good miniature presents, too.

## Mouse Theatre

Put your finger in the back of this mouse to make it creep along. To curl the card for its head and body, put it under a ruler, and pull it upward in a curve.

### What you need

....................................

Pink and white paper

Colored thread

Scissors

Ruler

Glue

Box

Colored tissue paper

### Finger mouse

**I** *Cut out a semicircle of pink paper and snip off one end. Cut a fringed strip of white paper with a red dot in the middle for the whiskers and nose. Cut out ears and eyes as shown.*

**2** *Fold the semicircle around and glue it to make a cone. Glue on the whiskers, eyes, and ears, as shown. Cut out a pink rectangle, fold it round, and glue it to make a body tube. Glue it behind the mouse's head and glue a curly tail to the back.*

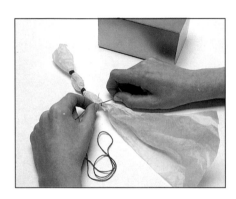

**I** *To transform a box into a stage, first paint it or cover it with paper. Then measure around the top and cut a slightly longer length of tissue paper. Tie thread around the paper at intervals, as shown, to make a row of tissue paper bunches. Fan out the paper a little between the threads.*

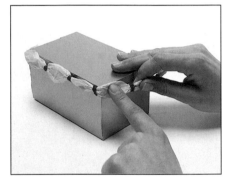

**2** *Use a thin paintbrush to dot glue onto the back of the pieces of thread along the tissue paper strip. Affix the strip to the outer top edge of the box for a theater stage decoration. You may need to do an edge at a time, making sure that it has stuck before going on to the next side.*

Hold the glued edges of the body and head together until they feel firm. Otherwise the edges may spring apart.

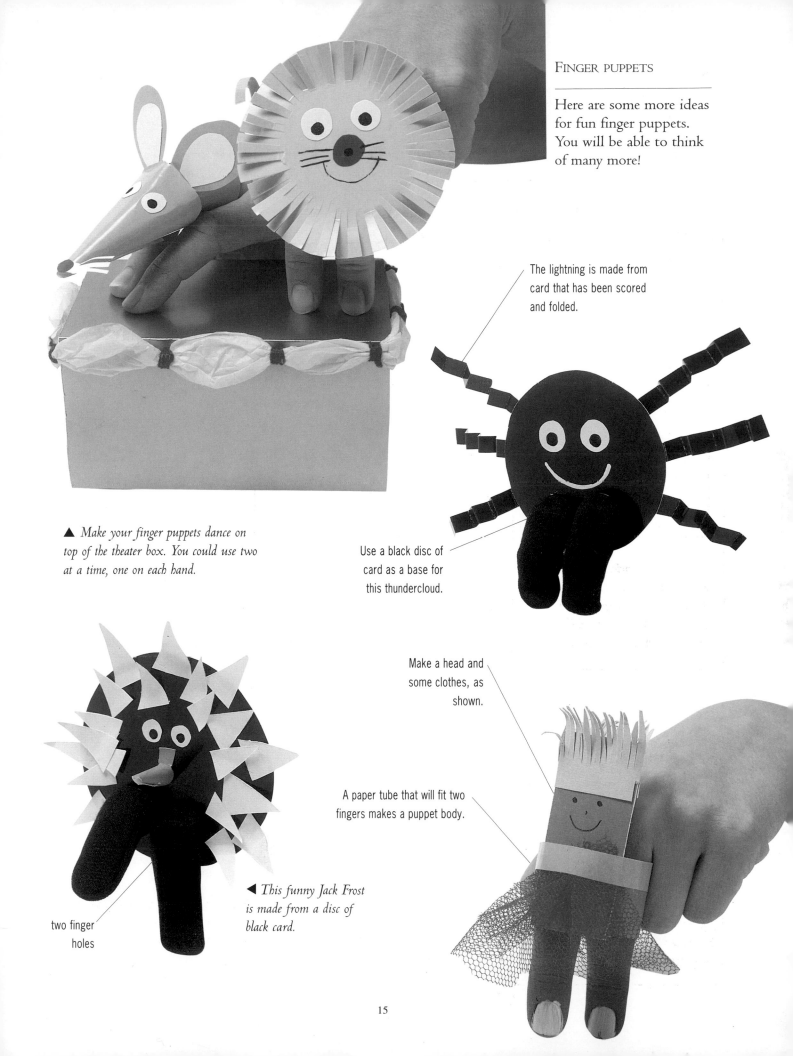

Here are some more ideas
for fun finger puppets.
You will be able to think
of many more!

The lightning is made from
card that has been scored
and folded.

Use a black disc of
card as a base for
this thundercloud.

▲ *Make your finger puppets dance on
top of the theater box. You could use two
at a time, one on each hand.*

Make a head and
some clothes, as
shown.

A paper tube that will fit two
fingers makes a puppet body.

two finger
holes

◄ *This funny Jack Frost
is made from a disc of
black card.*

15

# Stenciling

STENCILING IS A QUICK WAY TO make things look as if they have been printed. By cutting out simple shapes from card and dabbing paint through the holes, you can "print" patterns repeatedly. Then you can decorate all kinds of objects, such as envelopes, writing paper, cards, paper tablecloths, and even three-dimensional objects, such as boxes.

## PICTURE PATTERNS

A paper doily has pre-cut holes that make it ideal for stenciling patterns. Tape the doily on plain paper and dab different-colored paint over it.

Move the doily only when the paint is fully dry.

## MAKING STENCILS TO USE ON PAPER OR CARD

Follow the steps below to stencil on paper. Cut the stencils on an old tray and then use bright paint to transfer the shapes to colored paper.

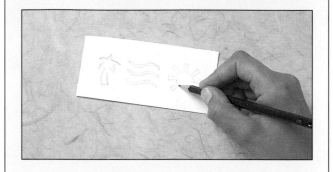

*1 Draw the shapes you want on card, spacing them out evenly for a clean, finished effect.*

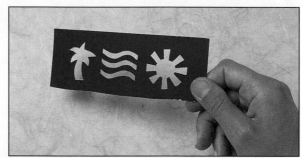

*2 Cut the shapes out carefully with a craft knife. Then position the card on the paper.*

*3 Using a stubby brush or a sponge, dab thick paint through the holes. Then carefully lift the card.*

## STENCILED STATIONERY

Here are some ideas for making stenciled stationery. You could stencil matching designs onto envelopes and writing paper to make your own personalized stationery set.

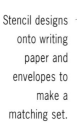

Stencil designs onto writing paper and envelopes to make a matching set.

Stencil round the edges of writing paper to make it look extra colorful.

Stencil party invitations with balloons or bows, or stencil a birthday card with the receiver's name.

# Stenciling ideas

Once you have practiced simple stencils, try making more complicated pictures using several different stencil shapes. The picture shown below is a "tree of life." You could glue a miniature calender at the bottom.

Try stenciling wrapping paper using a paint spray-can. You must do this outside, or in a place where it will not matter if the spray drifts onto other things.

## TREE OF LIFE

Start with a piece of thick cream or white cartridge paper. Use masking-tape to hold the edges down before you start painting. This will keep the page flat.

Cut different stencil shapes out of card - a pear, apple, bird, flowers, leaves, and a branch.

## SPRAY-CAN STENCILING

The paper below has been stenciled with a regular pattern of stars. This takes a long time to cut out, so you could start by trying a pattern that is simpler and more spaced out. You could try cutting out the letters of your name.

1 *Cut out a card shape that is slightly bigger than a rectangle of colored paper. Cut patterns out of the card. Then lie the card on top of the colored paper and tape round the edges.*

2 *Hold the paint spray-can away from the card and spray evenly all over. Leave the paint to dry and then peel away the card from the surface.*

Mix the different colored paints you need. Then gradually build up your picture by stenciling, in turn, the branches, then the leaves and flowers, then the apples and birds.

◀ *Cut out stencil shapes from the sides and lid of a cardboard box and line the inside with colored paper or shiny paper.*

Paint the box in your favorite color.

▼ *Make some wrapping paper with a pattern of your favorite animal on it, using a stencil you have made. Spray paint the stenciled pattern on, wearing rubber gloves.*

You can get different effects by spraying lightly in patches, or by spraying evenly all over.

# Papier Mache

Papier mache means "mashed paper" in French. This craft uses layers of paper which are soaked in glue and then stuck together to make attractive, usable objects. Papier mache has been used for centuries – it is surprisingly simple to make.

## Balloon Bowl

A papier mache bowl painted in bright patterns looks stunning. Paint the inside a different color.

1 *Cover your work surface with newspaper. Tape half a toilet-roll tube to the top of a blown-up balloon to hold it above the work surface. Rub petroleum jelly over the balloon. Tear newspaper strips about 1in (2cm) x 1.5in (4 cm), and dip them into the bowl of wallpaper paste.*

3 *Trim off the rough edges of the bowl. Paint the inside and, when this is dry, the outside of the bowl. Finish with a coat of varnish.*

▼ *Paint a picture on your papier mache bowl, as shown below, or dab paint onto a plain background with a clean sponge.*

2 *Stick the gluey paper strips to the top half of the balloon, overlapping them to make a bowl-shaped layer. When you have built up five or six layers, put the balloon and bowl somewhere warm to dry. After a day or two, the papier mache will be dry and hard. Pop the balloon and gently peel it away from the inside of the bowl.*

Always wait for one paint layer to dry before you paint another on top of it.

## BALLOON VASE

This colorful vase is made from a long balloon using the same method as for the bowl. The decorative top is made by attaching a ring of card to the top of the balloon, which is then covered with papier mache.

To display flowers inside your papier mache vase, put a glass jar inside to hold the water.

Try scrunching up the papier mache a little to create unusual shapes.

A coat of varnish will keep the dish well protected.

## PAPIER MACHE DISH

Clean polystyrene trays that form the backing for meat and vegetables can be recycled as a base for making your own imaginative dishes or trays. Build up five or six layers of papier mache on the front, back, and sides. Lay it on a sheet of polythene to dry.

# More papier mache

ONCE YOU HAVE MASTERED THE BASIC method of papier mache, you can make lots of decorative things. A mask or a funny party hat can be made using a balloon as a base, as shown on the previous pages. Since papier mache is so hard when dry, you can use it to make wall plaques as presents for your friends to hang on their bedroom walls.

## PAPIER MACHE MARACAS

To make some papier mache rattling maracas, first attach a toilet-roll tube to the top of a blown-up balloon with sticky tape. Cover the balloon and toilet-roll tube with strips of papier mache, as shown on the previous pages. Leave the end of the toilet-roll tube uncovered. When the papier mache is dry, pop the balloon, and fill the inside with dry beans, such as lentils or chick peas. Now, seal the end of the toilet-roll tube with some more papier mache. When dry, paint, and varnish the maraca.

Try putting different beans in each maraca. Large beans make a low sound, while smaller beans make a high sound.

*Pour the beans into the maraca through a plastic funnel, or make one from a rolled-up piece of card. Wait until the papier mache is dry first!*

Keep plaque shapes simple and paint the details on the dry surface with a thin paintbrush.

Make some flowers and hang them around a window for decoration.

## WALL PLAQUE

Draw an outline of a shape onto thick card (card from an empty packing box is ideal). Cut round the shape. Then build up layers of papier mache on top of it. While the papier mache is still wet, press into it with the end of a paintbrush to make lines. Mold parts of it with your fingers. When it is dry, paint and varnish it. Then, glue a loop of string to the back and hang it up on a wall.

### PRESERVING PAPIER MACHE
Always let papier mache dry thoroughly before you paint and varnish it. Ideally, leave it for a few days. Otherwise it could start to go moldy under the paint.

# Making boxes

IT IS EASY TO DECORATE BOXES AND MAKE THEM into extra-special gift containers. They're also ideal for hiding secrets in! Here are some simple ways to get started. Once you have tried these ideas, start designing your own personalized boxes.

## SIMPLE BOX

A square or rectangular box is the easiest shape to make at first. It is easiest to wrap, too!

### WHAT YOU NEED

A small empty box
(start saving them now!)

Scissors

Ruler

Pencil

Glue

Sheet of card

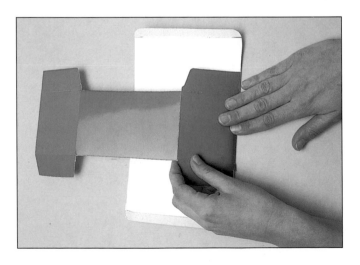

*1 Take the box carefully apart. You may need to ease a knife gently under any well-glued edges to help loosen them.*

*2 Place the flat box on a piece of card and draw round the edges, using a ruler to get them straight. Cut out this shape.*

*3 Score the edges that need to fold (see page 14 for more about scoring). Fold them in the same way as the original box.*

*4 Glue the edges in the same way as the original box. You may need to hold the edges together while they dry.*

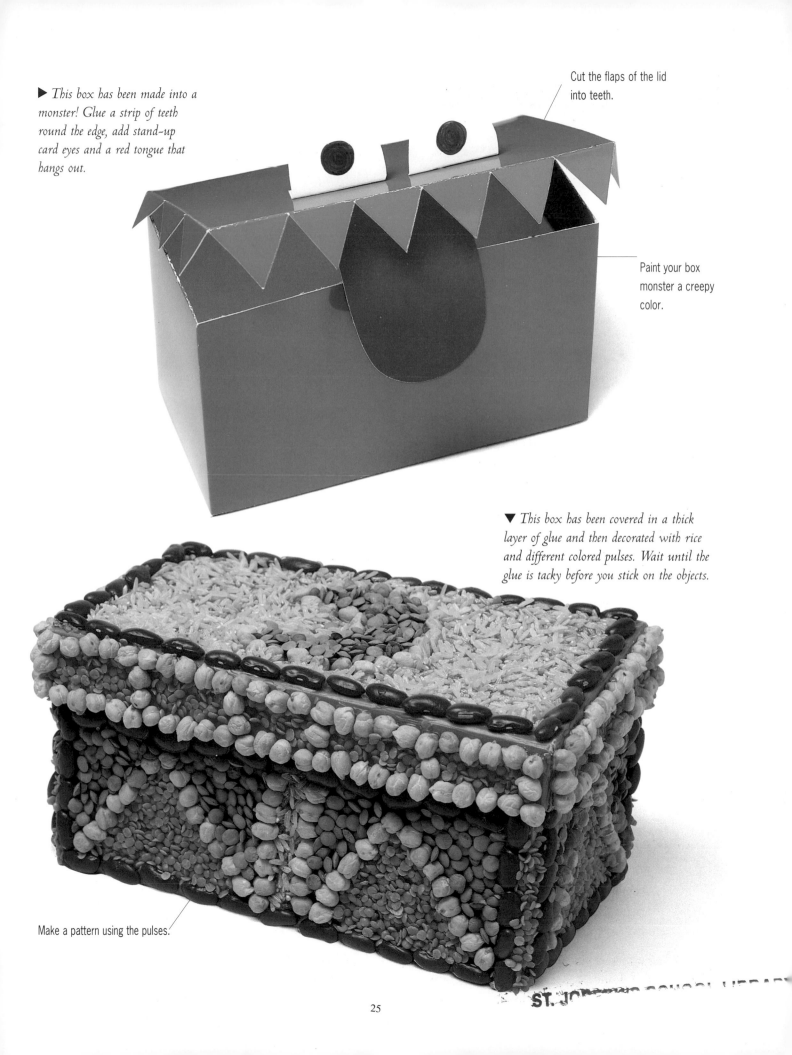

▶ *This box has been made into a monster! Glue a strip of teeth round the edge, add stand-up card eyes and a red tongue that hangs out.*

Cut the flaps of the lid into teeth.

Paint your box monster a creepy color.

▼ *This box has been covered in a thick layer of glue and then decorated with rice and different colored pulses. Wait until the glue is tacky before you stick on the objects.*

Make a pattern using the pulses.

# Box tricks

Here are some more fun ways to decorate a plain box. You may be able to think of some other variations of your own.

## POP-UP BOX

This box opens to reveal a hidden secret — a paper jumping jack! It is attached to the inside lid and base, and unfolds when the lid opens.

Cut a strip of paper about a third longer than the box depth. Fold it back and forth into a zigzag shape. Glue a card head with a smiley face on the top.

Glue the head to the inside lid, using a paper tab. Glue the other end of the zig-zag to the bottom of the box. The jumping jack will unfold when the lid is opened!

Decorate the outside of the box with bright paints or cut-out paper shapes.

Glue paper spirals to the inside lid so that they are hidden when the box lid is closed.

Make a matching gift tag for your box.

▼ *Buy interesting shaped boxes, or save any you are given, such as unusual chocolate boxes. Redecorate them by covering them with colored paper and cut-out paper shapes.*

Fill your box with homemade sweets for a special gift!

Peek through the holes at the object partially hidden inside.

▶ *Cut out shapes from the sides of a box. Then line it with different-colored paper, or put something interesting or unusual inside.*

# Decoupage

THE WORD DECOUPAGE COMES from the French word *decouper*, meaning "to cut." Cut-out printed images are glued to the surface of an object to decorate it. With decoupage you can use paper pictures to alter an ordinary household object into something unique and beautiful!

## WHAT YOU NEED

Small scissors
Pictures (from magazines, birthday cards, or wrapping paper)
Empty box
Paint
Glue
Clean cloth or sponge
Varnish

## GIFT BOX

Transform an ordinary box into a stunning gift box. Decorate it with colorful pictures cut from birthday cards, wrapping paper, or magazines.

1 *Paint the box all over, inside and out, with a bright color. This will be the background for the decoupage.*

2 *Cut out your chosen pictures. It is best to choose pictures with clear outlines so that you have easy edges to cut around.*

3 *Decide where to place your pictures to make an overall pattern or design. Brush glue over the back of each picture and firmly press it into position. Wipe off any extra glue with a clean cloth or sponge. Leave to dry and then varnish.*

The objects on this "fishy" box overlap to give a three-dimensional effect!

## PERFECT PLATES

Find a brightly colored paper plate. Stick on cut-out pictures from wrapping paper, either in the middle or around the outside, as a border. Varnish the plate and hang it on a wall.

Cut out a photograph of a pop star or sporting hero and stick it in the center of the plate. Surround the photo with cut-outs of suitable objects.

Think about the background color carefully before you start painting.

## COLORFUL BISCUIT TIN

Paint an empty biscuit tin with emulsion paint. When the paint is thoroughly dry, stick decoupage shapes or objects over it. This one has been made using pictures from old-fashioned wrapping paper on a deep red background.

When positioning the decoupage cut-outs, remember you can allow some of the background color to show through as part of the design.

◄ *This heart-shaped brooch is made from card, with a safety-pin glued or taped on the back.*

Add decoupage, matching ribbons, and lace.

# Book ends

Iℕ 18ᴛʜ ᴄᴇɴᴛᴜʀʏ Fʀᴀɴᴄᴇ ᴀɴᴅ Iᴛᴀʟʏ decoupage was used to cover all sorts of household objects, including furniture. You can do the same by making a pair of book ends from card. The ones shown here have been decorated with flowers cut out from birthday wrapping paper.

YOU WILL NEED

Two rectangles of card 14in (35.5cm)
x 7in (18cm)
Two small boxes 5in (12.5cm)
x 2.5in (6cm) x 3in (7.5cm)
Plasticine
Paint and brushes
Glue and scissors
Varnish
Decorative wrapping paper sheets

## Fʟᴏʀᴀʟ ʙᴏᴏᴋ ᴇɴᴅs

A pair of decoupage book ends would look great propping up your books. For extra decoration, cut out interesting shapes from the card tops, following the shapes made by the decoupage pieces.

Cover each box with decoupage.

You could cut pieces from such souces as magazines, greetings cards, or wrapping paper.

1 Measure a third of the way up the card rectangles and draw a line across each one. Score along these lines (see page 14) and bend them into an "L" shape. Paint the cards and boxes.

2 When dry, glue decoupage pieces all over them. Then put a couple of handfuls of plasticine inside each box to weigh them down and glue the boxes into the card corners.

This extra decorated card slots into the the top of the box.

▲ *If your book ends are pushed over by your books, you can make them heavier by putting more plasticine inside the boxes. Alternatively you could fill them with stones.*

## DECOUPAGE SPOON

Paint a wooden spoon a bright colour. While it is drying, carefully cut out pictures and stick them in a pattern over the spoon.

Stick large bright flowers on the head, with smaller flowers on the handle.

Hang the decorated spoon in your kitchen with string.

# Marbling

MARBLING PRODUCES BEAUTIFUL patterned papers, each one unique. Part of the fun is that each time you marble, the effect will be different and completely unpredictable! Although marbling is much easier than it looks, it is a messy process, so wear an apron and rubber gloves.

## WHAT YOU NEED

Apron and rubber gloves

Oil-based paints, watered down with white spirit if they are too thick

Shallow baking tray

Thick cartridge paper, cut to fit in the baking tray

Vinegar

Newspaper

Paintbrushes

Cocktail sticks

Masking tape

## MARBLING ON PAPER

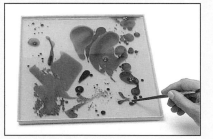  

**1** Fill the tray almost to the brim with water. Mix in a generous splash of vinegar. If your paints are thick, water them down with white spirit to make them runny. Use a paintbrush to dribble and flick different colors onto the water surface. They should float. Swirl the colours gently round with a cocktail stick.

**2** Lay the paper on the water surface, so it lies flat. Tap over it very gently with your finger to get rid of any air bubbles underneath. Air bubbles spoil the marble pattern by causing big white blobs. Leave the paper on the surface for a few moments.

**3** Lift up the paper with both hands, holding onto either side. Hold it above the tray to let any excess water drain off. Then, lay the paper face-up on some newspaper and attach masking tape on either side to hold the sheet down flat while it dries.

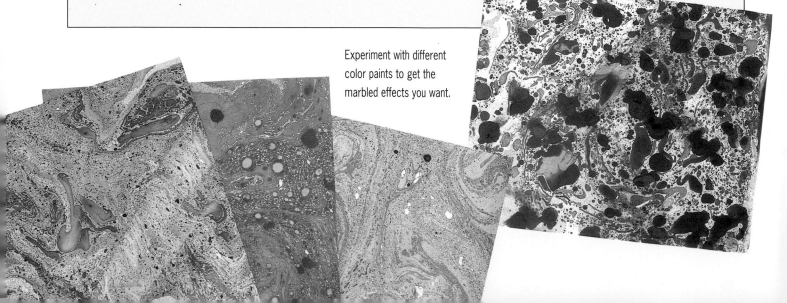

Experiment with different color paints to get the marbled effects you want.

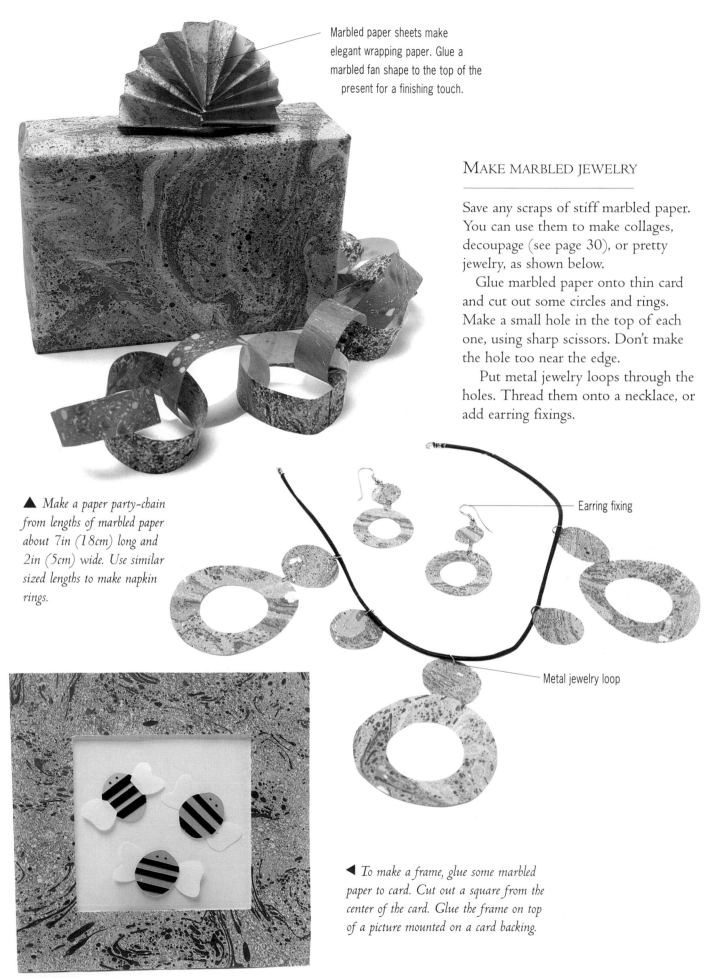

Marbled paper sheets make elegant wrapping paper. Glue a marbled fan shape to the top of the present for a finishing touch.

## MAKE MARBLED JEWELRY

Save any scraps of stiff marbled paper. You can use them to make collages, decoupage (see page 30), or pretty jewelry, as shown below.

Glue marbled paper onto thin card and cut out some circles and rings. Make a small hole in the top of each one, using sharp scissors. Don't make the hole too near the edge.

Put metal jewelry loops through the holes. Thread them onto a necklace, or add earring fixings.

▲ *Make a paper party-chain from lengths of marbled paper about 7in (18cm) long and 2in (5cm) wide. Use similar sized lengths to make napkin rings.*

Earring fixing

Metal jewelry loop

◄ *To make a frame, glue some marbled paper to card. Cut out a square from the center of the card. Glue the frame on top of a picture mounted on a card backing.*

33

# Marbled book covers

TRADITIONALLY, MARBLED PAPER is used to cover books to make them look attractive and to protect them. Here is an easy way to make a loose jacket for your favorite book, and to make a matching book plate with your name on it. The book plate goes inside a book, on the first page.

### WHAT YOU NEED

Rectangle of thin marbled paper large enough to wrap around the book with some to spare

Scissors

Marbled paper for the bookplate

Ruler and pencil

Glue

## BOOK JACKET

1 *Measure a book from top to bottom. Using your ruler and a pencil, mark this length on the back of the marbled paper, and trim it to fit.*

2 *Measure round the book from cover to cover, including the spine. Using your ruler and pencil, mark this width on the inside of the jacket paper, allowing an extra margin of 2in (5cm) on either side.*

3 *Trim the jacket to the right size and then fold it carefully round the book as shown. If you like, trim the inside folds to a wavy shape, or cut out a hole in the front of the jacket to show some of the book title beneath.*

## BOOK PLATE

Measure the front page of a book you want to decorate. Draw a rectangle the same size on the back of the marbled paper and cut it out. Cut a rectangle of plain white thick paper the same size.

Measure and mark a line 1in (2.5cm) all round the inside edge of the marbled rectangle. Cut round the line to make a frame and glue it on top of the plain paper rectangle.

Write on the plain paper, "This book belongs to ..." and then your name and the date. To help you to write in a straight line, draw some faint pencil lines with a ruler, then rub them out after you have written along them. Glue the book plate into your book.

▶ *Cover precious diaries, address books, and cookbooks. Not only will they look special, they will be protected by the marbled paper, too.*

Have fun experimenting with different color mixes. Try bright, contrasting mixes or subtle, pale ones.

# Making books

CREATE A UNIQUE MASTERPIECE! MAKE YOUR own book, write a story inside, and illustrate it. Books come in lots of different shapes and sizes. Here are a few suggestions to try, but look in your own book collection for other ideas.

WHAT YOU NEED
..........................
A4 or A3 sheets of cartridge
paper
Large needle
Strong thread
Masking tape

## SEWN BOOK

Here is a simple way to make the inside pages of a small book.

1 *Take three or four sheets of paper (you will find it hard to sew through more than that). Fold each page carefully in half, as shown. Then, lay the pages inside each other, so that all the edges line up. To help keep them in place, you could fold some small pieces of masking tape over the edges. You can take these off later.*

2 *Thread the needle and knot one end. Sew up the middle of the book, pushing the needle through to the back and then to the front. Sew up to the top and down to the bottom; then repeat this to make the book really strong. When you have finished, knot the thread on the inside and trim the loose end.*

## CONCERTINA BOOK

This concertina book has been decorated with holiday photos, painted shapes, and cut-out paper pieces. You could write a holiday diary on the other side to keep as a souvenir. To make the book, take a long piece of plain card. Measure and mark it to make three equal-sized sections. Score along the lines (see page 14).

Score one line down one side of the card and the other line down the other side, so that one section folds back and the other folds forward. Flatten the book into a squashed zigzag shape with your hand.

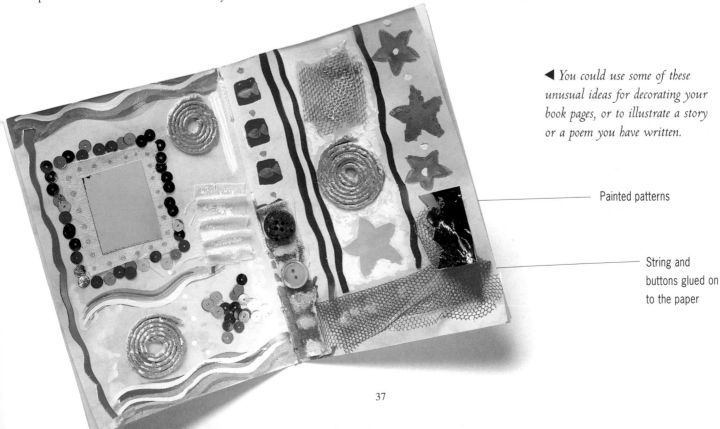

◀ *You could use some of these unusual ideas for decorating your book pages, or to illustrate a story or a poem you have written.*

— Painted patterns

— String and buttons glued on to the paper

# Book covers

Here are some unusual book covers to make. Each one you do will be a unique personal design – the only one in the world!

## WOVEN BOOK COVER

Draw a simple shape, such as a heart, on the cover of one of your home-made books. Make holes around the shape's outline using a needle. Then, weave colored thread through the holes from top to bottom. Decorate the edges of the book with different colored thread, as shown.

## FOLDER COVER

Decorate a project folder cover with a picture that shows the theme of the project. Here, a fish suggests a sea theme.

◄ *You could sew the pages of your book together using holes made with a needle and a piece of thread. There are many ways to do this so that the binding is a decorative feature of the book. It is best not to use too many pages though; three or four sheets a time is usually enough.*

## SPECIAL RING-BINDER COVER

If you have a ring-binder that you use for a special project, you could decorate its cover. Try gluing on pasta or dry kidney beans to give the cover a three-dimensional look.

Coat the cover of the ring-binder with glue and stick the pasta shapes on it in patterns and lines. Use dry kidney beans to decorate the spine, or try another kind of pasta shape.

When the glue is dry, put the binder on some newspaper and spray with a can of silver or gold paint. Or cover parts of the binder with masking tape to add different colored patterns.

Instead of using pasta shells, try sticking on shells for a seaside theme!

# Making mobiles

A MOBILE IS A MOVING SCULPTURE where hanging objects are carefully balanced from a frame. So long as they are correctly balanced you can use almost any object – but remember to think about what they will look like when viewed from underneath and from all sides.

### SPIRAL MOBILE

Try this easy mobile to start with. It is based on a spiral made from colored card.

<table>
<tr><td colspan="1" align="center">WHAT YOU NEED</td></tr>
<tr><td align="center">

Circle of card, 6in (15cm) diameter

String, wool, or strong embroidery thread cut into four 4in (10cm) thread lengths

Plain card scraps

Paint

Brush

Scissors

</td></tr>
</table>

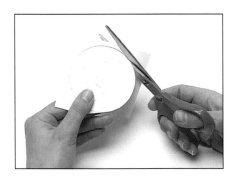

1 Cut a spiral from the card circle and make four holes along the length. Paint and cut out four shapes of about the same size. Make a hole in the top of each one.

2 Push a length of thread through each hole and knot the end to secure it. Knot the other ends through the holes in the spiral. Hang the mobile up with thread.

Hang smaller shapes from the larger ones, experimenting to get the right balance.

## NATURAL MOBILE

Find natural objects, such as shells and pebbles, to hang from a mobile. This mobile is made from a starfish shell, but you could get a similar effect using a coathanger.

Begin by covering a coathanger with pretty strips of material. Then, either make holes in the shells with a needle and push through the thread, or simply tie the thread around the shells. You could also use buttons and beads. Then hang everything from the coathanger.

---

### WHAT YOU NEED
.......................................

Natural objects,
such as shells and pebbles
Beads and buttons
Strong thread
Needle
Coathanger
Pretty rags

---

◀ *This mobile works because the starfish shape is symmetrical, which means its shape is balanced all round. See if you can think of other symmetrical shapes you could use for the main part of a mobile!*

Hang small, light objects near the top of the thread, and large, heavy ones at the bottom.

# Mobile tricks

WHEN YOU DESIGN A MOBILE, choose hanging objects that will look effective swinging in the air above your head.

## SPIDER'S WEB

Making this web takes care and time, but the result is very unusual. If you want, leave out the web and hang just the spiders from the frame.

To secure the spiders, knot the middle of the thread around the frame and tie the top ends together.

1 *Lay the three sticks in a star shape and tie them tightly round the middle. Try to keep them spaced evenly as you do this by weaving the thread over and over between the sticks.*

2 *Now, weave another length of thread round the sticks, moving outwards. Knot the thread at the end. Hang the spiders from the sticks, running each thread up above the frame to hang the mobile and keep it level.*

## SPACE MOBILE

This outer-space mobile glints and glitters in the light! The objects hang from a thick cardboard star shape, covered with silver foil. Don't forget to balance the objects so the mobile hangs evenly from the ceiling!

The planets are made from painted polystyrene balls – cut one ball in half to make martians!

Make a spaceship from a toilet-roll tube, covering it with silver foil, or painting it.

You could use silver thread to complete the shiny effect.

### WHAT YOU NEED

Thick card

Polystyrene balls

toilet-roll tube

Glue

Silver foil

Glitter

Paint

Brush

Silver or black thread

Scissors

Tiny bells (optional)

Stars and moons can be cut out from card and painted.

◄ *Your space mobile will jangle in the breeze if you can find some tiny bells to hang on it.*

Tiny bell

### ADDING EXTRA SPARKLE
Dab on glue to add glitter to the space objects.

# Tie-dyeing

USE TIE-DYEING TO MAKE STRIPY or swirly patterns, and other exciting effects, on plain-colored T-shirts, bags, hats, and even pillow-cases and sheets! You can buy small packets of dye to use. Make sure it is cold dye, which does not need hot water to make it work. Follow the dyeing instructions given by the manufacturer.

## STRIPY RINGS

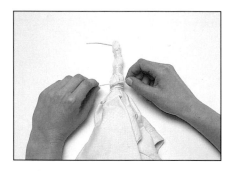

1 Lie the T-shirt flat and pull it up from the middle. Tie string round it at intervals. The dye will not reach the places covered by the string.

2 Mix the dye as directed on the packet. Use a bowl to hold the dye, and place over newspaper. Immerse the T-shirt in the dye. The longer you leave it, the darker the color will be.

3 Take the T-shirt out of the dye and put it in a sink. Rinse it in cold water, after removing the string. Then, when you have washed, dried, and ironed it, your new colorful T-shirt is ready to wear!

This T-shirt was tie-dyed using the stripy ring method.

## PLEATING

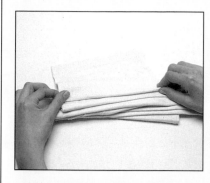 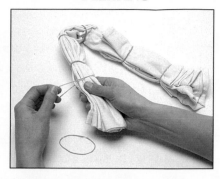 

$I$ Mix the dye, as instructed on the packet. Starting at the top, fold the T-shirt into pleats backwards and forwards until you get one long zigzag sausage shape.

$2$ Tie string or rubber bands at intervals along the sausage shape to hold it securely. Then, immerse it in the bowl of dye.

$3$ Leave the sausage shape for the time specified on the packet. Then, put it in a sink, snip off the string or rubber bands, and rinse until the water runs clear. Wash, dry, and iron.

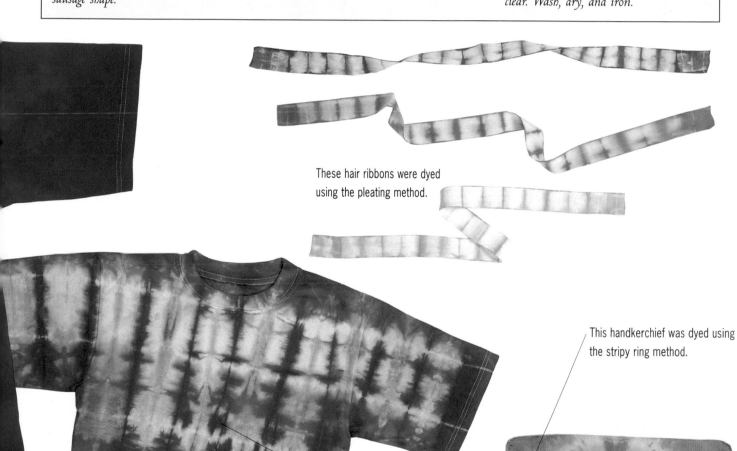

These hair ribbons were dyed using the pleating method.

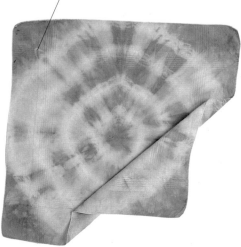

This handkerchief was dyed using the stripy ring method.

The pleating method, shown above, produced the vibrant colors on this T-shirt.

# Swirls and circles

Here are two more tie-dyeing patterns to try. The swirling technique creates a stunning multi-colored pattern, while stone-tying creates miniature circles with blobs in the middle. It is a good idea to practice both methods on some old rags first, before you dye a more important object. The list on the previous page shows you what equipment you need. For swirling, you also need some wide brushes.

▶ *This brightly colored T-shirt was dyed using the swirling technique.*

---

## SWIRLING

1 *Lie your garment flat and pick it up by the middle. Twist it round into a spiral. Put two rubber bands over the spiral to keep it in place.*

2 *Separately mix four different-colored dyes into thick pastes. Then, paint a quarter of the spiral with each color.*

3 *Turn the bundle over and paint each quarter on the other side the same color as before. Put the bundle in a plastic bag, seal it with a rubber band, and leave it overnight.*

4 *Snip off the rubber bands and rinse the garment until the water runs clean. Then, wash, dry, and iron it. Now you have a stunning multi colored swirl!*

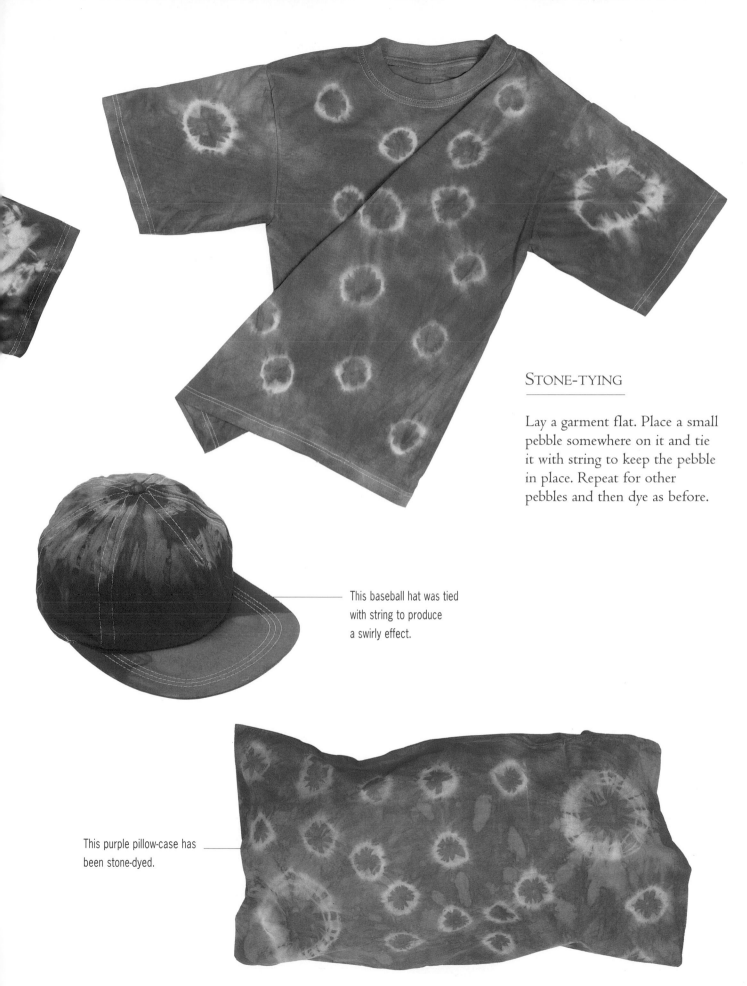

## STONE-TYING

Lay a garment flat. Place a small pebble somewhere on it and tie it with string to keep the pebble in place. Repeat for other pebbles and then dye as before.

This baseball hat was tied with string to produce a swirly effect.

This purple pillow-case has been stone-dyed.

# Fabric painting

USE FABRIC PAINTS AND PENS TO decorate your clothes and wear the art you have made! Use them to personalize some of the furnishings in your bedroom, too. Buy brush-on fabric paint to color large areas, and use fabric paints for writing and to add bold outlines to shapes.

## CLOTHES ART

Start with a plain piece of clothing, such as a T-shirt, vest, hat, or pair of shorts, and end up with an exciting, unique piece of fashion art!

*1 Wash and dry the garment. While it is drying, plan what you are going to paint or draw. Sketch your designs on paper. Perhaps use a theme, such as a "holiday scene" or "my name."*

### WHAT YOU NEED

Plain cotton garments
Fabric paints or pens
Paint brush
Old shirt,
to protect clothes
Newspaper,
to protect surfaces
Large plastic bag

*2 Iron the garment and lie it on newspaper. If you are using a T-shirt, put a large plastic bag inside so that when you decorate the front the paint does not stain the back. When painting your design, start by painting the light colors and then move on to the dark colors.*

*3 Let your paint or pen drawing dry. Follow the manufacturer's instructions to fix the colors. You may need to lie a cloth over the paint and then iron over it.*

You could make a special design for a friend or a relative's birthday.

Look for design inspiration from things you collect on holiday, such as this starfish.

▼ *Personalize a clothing design to fit a particular person. Use their name, their star-sign, or their favorite hobby as a theme.*

ANNA

▼ *Shorts decorated in lively patterned rows.*

▲ *Summer hat, with the brim adorned with flowers on a green background.*

◄ *A spider's web handkerchief.*

# Fabric paint projects

HERE ARE SOME DIFFERENT WAYS TO APPLY FABRIC paints, and some projects to try. Do not forget that you can mix fabric paints together to get new shades, just like you can with ordinary paints.

## DECORATING A SCARF

Find a long piece of plain cotton material to make a scarf. Print on it, and add freehand painting, too, if you like.

1 *Iron your material and lay it on newspaper, or a plastic bag. Cut a potato in half and use a sharp knife to cut a shape into the surface — or if you'd rather, just leave it round. As an alternative, you could use sponges cut into shapes (you can buy these from toy shops).*

2 *Pour a little fabric paint into a shallow dish and dip the potato or sponge into it. Press the printing shape onto some scrap paper. Experiment with the method before trying it on your scarf.*

Choose a fabric paint color that will show up on the background you have chosen.

This scarf has a seam sewn around it to stop it from fraying.

50

## BEDROOM BANNER

This hanging fabric banner would look great in your room.

### WHAT YOU NEED

......................................

Length of plain cotton material

Pinking shears (to make a zigzag cut)

Needle and thread

Two pieces of dowelling

Colored cord

Glue, pencil, and ruler

Cut out your cotton fabric strip using pinking shears (this will stop the edges from fraying). If you want to disguise crooked edges, cut shapes into them. Lay the strip on newspaper, or a plastic bag.

Use fabric paints or pens to decorate the banner. Leave the strip to dry and follow any paint instructions for fixing colors.

Turn the banner over to the back. Use a pencil and ruler to mark a line 1.5in (4cm) from the top and bottom.

Paint a thin line of glue along the top and turn the banner edge over to make a tunnel. Do the same along the bottom line.

When the glue is dry, slip the dowelling into the seams. Tie the cord round the top dowelling to hang the banner.

Stick on sequins, or sew on beads.

If you like, stick other scraps of material, such as felt, to your banner to create a collage effect.

# Simple batik

Batik is a method of fabric painting that is traditional in Asia. It produces brightly-colored patterns and shapes, usually with a white outline. Traditional batik is hard to do because it involves the use of hot wax. Here is an easy way to get the same effect using a mixture of flour and water.

## WHAT YOU NEED

White cotton fabric
(try starting with a simple square shape)

Fabric paints

Flour and water

Paint brushes

Old shirt, to protect clothes

Plastic bag, to protect any surfaces

Paper and crayons for doing
a rough design

Cleaned-out washing-up liquid bottle

## BATIK SNAKE PICTURE

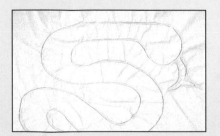

*1 Mix the flour and water to make a runny dough. Stretch out the fabric on top of a plastic bag. If you want, tape the edges down with masking tape. Unscrew the top of the washing-up bottle and pour the flour and water mix into it through a funnel.*

*2 Screw the top back on the bottle and paint patterns with it, or outline a shape, on the fabric. Leave the dough to dry overnight. When dry, use fabric paints to cover in the areas inbetween the dough lines.*

*3 When the paint has dried, pick off the dough with your fingers and watch your batik design emerge. You will find that the fabric under the dough has stayed white. Fix the paint colors using the manufacturer's instructions.*

◀ *Here's the finished snake picture. You could try patterns instead of a picture, or even random shapes, on your fabric. Your mistakes usually just add to the originality of your work!*

Wild designs, such as this, could enliven a cushion cover or a T-shirt.

53

# Batik clothes

THE SIMPLE BATIK EFFECT WORKS WELL ON clothes. Treat it in the same way as you would ordinary fabric painting (see page 50). The bikini top shown here can double-up as a bandana. The hair scrunchy can be adapted to make hair ribbons.

## HAIR SCRUNCHY

Use really bright colors to make this scrunchy stand out.

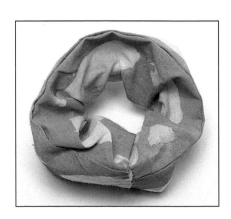

### WHAT YOU NEED

Two strips of plain cotton fabric, both 1.5in (4cm) x 7in (18cm)

Length of elastic, 3.5in (9cm)

Needle and thread

Fabric paints

Prepared bottle of flour and water mix

Plastic bag

Pinking shears

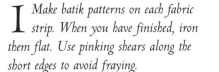

1 *Make batik patterns on each fabric strip. When you have finished, iron them flat. Use pinking shears along the short edges to avoid fraying.*

2 *Lay the patterned sides together and put pins along either side. Sew a seam along either side.*

3 *Turn the strip inside-out and thread the elastic through. Pull the elastic tight and knot the ends together. The fabric will scrunch up into a ball.*

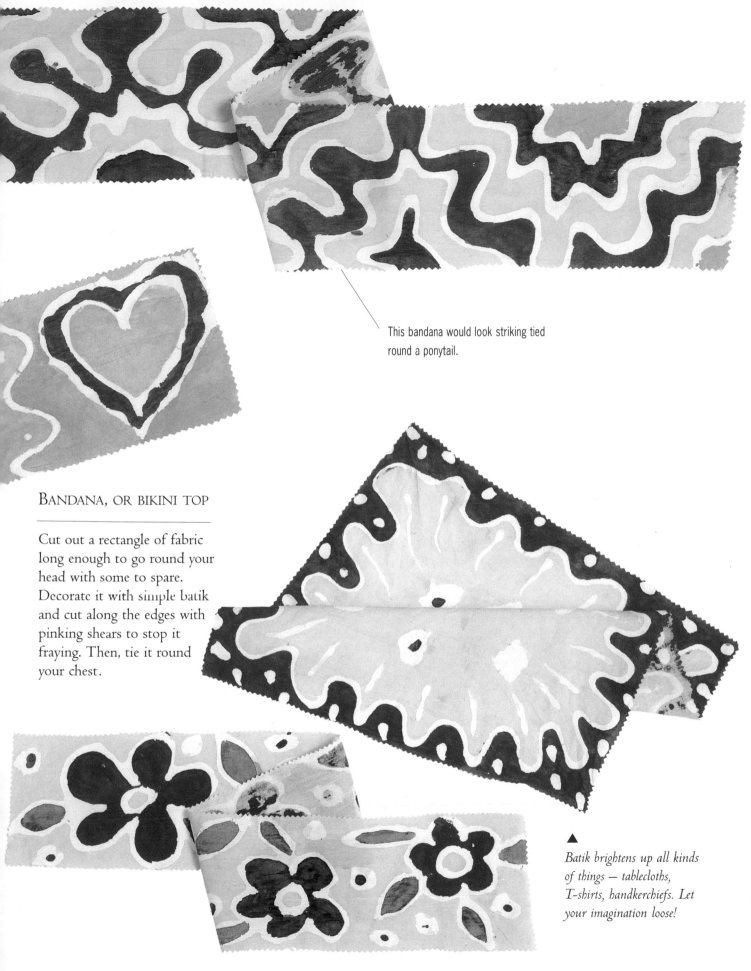

This bandana would look striking tied round a ponytail.

## BANDANA, OR BIKINI TOP

Cut out a rectangle of fabric long enough to go round your head with some to spare. Decorate it with simple batik and cut along the edges with pinking shears to stop it fraying. Then, tie it round your chest.

▲

*Batik brightens up all kinds of things — tablecloths, T-shirts, handkerchiefs. Let your imagination loose!*

# Starting patchwork

PATCHWORK IS A TRADITIONAL CRAFT that has been practiced for centuries. It is a good way to use up scraps of pretty material (if you enjoy it, start keeping a bag of scraps for future use). In this book, you can learn how to begin with the easiest patchwork shape – a square. If you become an expert, you could start trying other shapes.

## PATCHWORK PLAN

Start by making a card template as a model for the fabric squares you make. Then plan your patchwork on graph, or squared, paper. Color in the squares the way you want and number the rows, starting at the top and going down.

Making a patchwork plan before you start will let you see how your patchwork should look when complete.

### WHAT YOU NEED

Cotton fabric pieces, 5in (12.5cm) x 5in (12.5cm), washed and ironed

Scrap card (empty cereal packets will do)

Ruler, scissors, and pencil

Crayons and squared paper, or graph paper

Water-soluble fabric pen, or dressmaker's chalk

Medium-size needle and thread

## SQUARE-MAKING

1 Draw a square 5in (12.5cm)x 5in (12.5cm) on card. Draw another square inside the first one, 0.5in (1cm) smaller all round. Accuracy is important, so measure carefully.

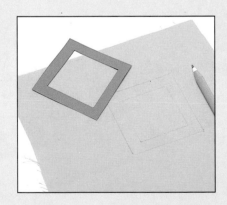

2 Cut out the center square, leaving a square template with a square hole in the middle. Put your template on the underside of a piece of fabric from which you intend to cut out a patchwork piece.

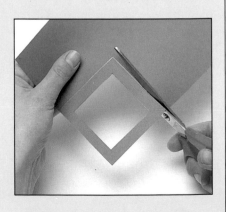

3 Mark carefully round the inside and outside with your water-soluble fabric pen or dressmaker's chalk. Cut round the outside square line you have made. Cut as many different fabric squares as you need.

Checkerboard patterns –
using just two colors, a
light and a dark one – look
particularly striking.

Put your different-colored fabric
squares in separate piles until you
need them.

57

# Making patchwork

THE INSTRUCTIONS BELOW ARE FOR making patchwork using handsewing. Follow the same steps on a sewing machine if you can use one. On the right, there are some suggestions for making objects out of patchwork.

Doll's quilt.

## BASIC PATCHWORK

1 Start with two squares from the top row of your plan. Pin their right sides together. Knot one end of your thread and use small running stitches (a line of even-length stitches) to sew along one of the inner square lines. Oversew the same stitch twice and then cut the thread.

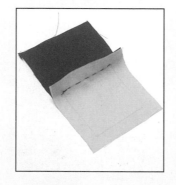

2 Attach the next square in the row by sewing it in the same way. Keep going until a row is done; then iron all the seams open. Make the other rows in your plan the same way. It may help to pin a label to each finished row to tell you what number it is on your paper plan.

3 Lay one row on another, right sides together with all the seams matching. Pin along the length and sew all the way along one side. Continue until you have finished your plan. Then iron the seams out flat.

## DOLL'S QUILT

To make a pretty quilt for a doll, make sure your patchwork is big enough for a doll's bed. Cut a piece of plain fabric to the same size and pin it to the back of the patchwork, matching the edges. Sew along each side about 1in (2.5cm) from the edge. Then use pinking shears to trim round the quilt (this will make the edges crinkly and stops them fraying).

Easy bag

## EASY BAG

Make one long piece of patchwork.
Sew some material to the back to
strengthen it if you wish (see the
doll's quilt). Use pinking shears
along either side and then fold it
in half, with the right sides
together, and sew up each side.
Turn about 0.75in (2cm) over
around the top; turn it
again, and then sew along
this edge to keep it in place.
Turn the bag rightside out and
iron it. Stitch a piece of cord inside the
bag to make a handle.

A miniature
version of the
bag without the
cord provides a
special
patchwork case.

A square
version of the
doll's quilt can
be used
as a table mat.

# Friendship bracelets

$\mathbf{Y}$OU CAN MAKE BEAUTIFUL BRACELETS by using simple knotting techniques. It does not take long to become an expert, and it is possible to make this craft anywhere, at any time! Wear the bracelets round your wrist or knot them into your hair. Personalize them by using your favourite colors.

## SETTING UP

You need different-colored embroidery threads. Knot them together with a 6in (15cm) tassel above the knot. Then secure the knot by a safety pin onto a cushion on your knee. When you become an expert, you may be able to do it with the knot pinned to the knee of your jeans!

---

## WHAT YOU NEED

Two 27.5in (70cm) strands of thread of one color

Two 27.5in (70cm) strands of thread of another color

Safety pin

Cushion

---

## MAKING A BRACELET

**1** *Knot the threads together (see "setting up".) Spread them out with two same-colored threads on the left and the other two on the right. Lift the left-hand thread and bring it over the one next to it, on the right.*

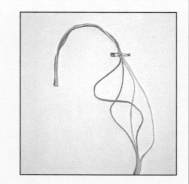

**2** *Tuck the first thread back underneath and round over the other thread again, making an S shape, as shown. Then slide the first thread up to the top and pull it to make a tight knot. Do these two steps again so you end up with two knots.*

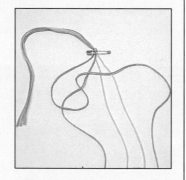

**3** *Move the thread on the left out of the way and repeat the first two steps using the next two threads along. Repeat for all threads. You will then have made a whole row of knots. Make more rows, starting each time with the thread lying on the left.*

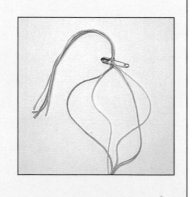

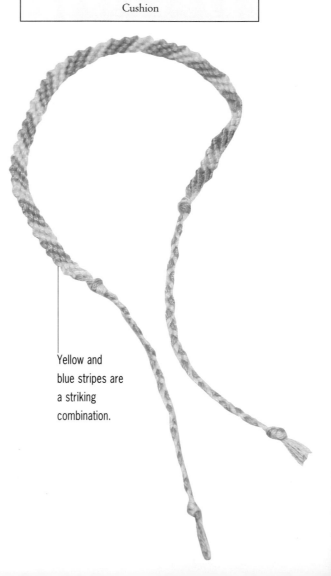

Yellow and blue stripes are a striking combination.

## FINISHING OFF

When you get to the end of a striped section, tie all the threads in a knot. Then, unpin the bracelet from the cushion and finish the tassels by plaiting or beading them.

The easiest way to complete the tassels is to plait them together, tie them in a knot at the end and trim them near the knot. Put the two middle strands together and plait them as one thread.

If you want, plait the tassels, tie a knot, thread on a large bead and tie another knot to keep it in place. Or leave each tassel free and tie a small bead to the end of each one. Then, place your bracelet on your wrist.

You could hang friendship bracelets in your hair, as well as wearing them on your wrist.

Look for big, bright, wooden beads to use on bracelets.

## PLAITING

Instead of knotting, you could do a simple plaited bracelet. Use two threads together as a plaiting strand. That way, your bracelet will be thick and bold-looking. Knot the threads as before and pin them to a cushion. Then, always working with the strand on the left, go over, under, over, under the threads to the right.

Don't tighten your knots too much or leave them too loose. You will learn what tension is best by practicing.

Try plaiting three, four, five, and even six strands. The bracelet will be thicker each time.

61

# Macrame and more

MACRAME IS THE ART OF TYING knots in patterns. It is simple and quick to do, and you can make all kinds of colorful bracelets.

Try making plaited bracelets using colored string, strips of colored braid, or ribbon.

## MACRAME BRACELET

This bracelet uses two different-colored sets of threads – four strands of the same color down the middle (the "filler" threads) and two pairs of threads on either side (the "worker" threads), in the second color.

### WHAT YOU NEED

Four filler strands, 20in (51cm) long

Four worker strands 27.5in (70cm) long

Safety pin

Cushion

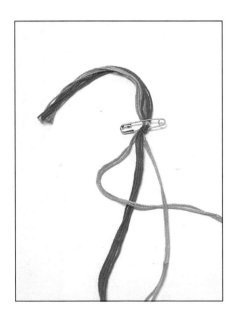

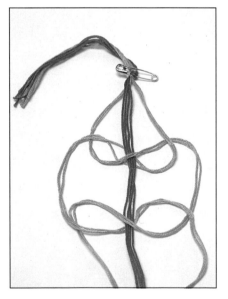

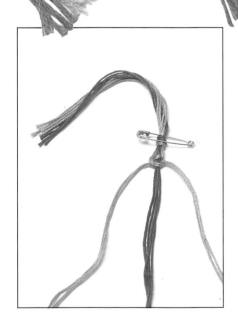

1 Tie the threads together with a 4in (10cm) tassel and pin the knot on a cushion with the fillers in the middle and the workers either side. Use the pair of workers together, as if they were a single strand. Put the left-hand workers over the fillers and under the right-hand workers.

2 Put the right-hand workers under the fillers and over the left-hand workers. Then, pick up the workers which are now on the left and put them under the fillers and over the workers, which are now on the right. Put these right-hand workers up over the fillers and through the loop on the left-hand side, as shown.

3 Pull on both sets of workers gently, to tighten the knots you have made. Repeat the process until your bracelet is the length you want. Then, tie all the threads together in a knot and finish the bracelet tassels how you like.

To tie a bracelet securely, use a reef knot – right end over left end and under, then left end over right end and under.

Make a plain-colored bracelet, using the method on page 62 for stripy bracelets. Then, sew beads onto the bracelet to decorate it.

◀ *Your bracelet will look bright if you use a mixture of colors that contrast well with each other. Do not forget that black and white are a stunning combination, and yellow looks great with blue, green, or red.*

# Collage

COLLAGE IS THE ART OF MAKING a picture by putting together lots of different materials because of their interesting colors, shapes, or textures. You can put almost anything on a collage providing you can glue it down successfully.

1 Paint a colorful background on your piece of card. This picture has a green background with yellow spots on.

2 Paint a thick layer of glue all over the inside of the shape. Stick pulses, beans, and rice on it to make different-colored areas. Think about using the shapes of the pulses. For instance, kidney beans make a good beak on this picture of a rooster.

3 You can add paint as well, if you like. This rooster's tail feathers are made from orange split peas, and pulses, which have been painted pink. The body is rice, painted yellow.

## COLLAGE PICTURE TILE

Mount this miniature picture on a larger mirror tile, or a piece of different-colored card.

Make several different animals on squares of card. Then, display them next to each other.

Here's an unusual valentine, made using beans and pulses.

# COLLAGE ART

Choose collage materials carefully to get the effect you want. Here are some examples of different styles to try.

Green lentils

Kidney beans

Red lentils

*◀ Stick collage pieces onto a papier mache bowl or pot. This one was covered with a thick layer of glue and then decorated with different-colored pulses.*

*▼ To brighten up a flower pot, stick buttons and beads all round it.*

*▶ If you break up an eggshell and stick it on a papier mache bowl, it cracks in an interesting way, but won't fall apart.*

*▲ This pot is covered with pieces of eggshell, spray-painted silver.*

# Collage frames

Here are some more ways to make collage displays. The collage picture frame uses shells, but you can use anything with an interesting shape or color. The silver pictures are pulses sprayed with a can. Collage can also be used to make three-dimensional displays.

These tiles are made in a similar way to those shown on page 66, but these have been sprayed silver.

Make a hook for the back of your collage frame to hang it on your wall.

1 Cut out a frame from a piece of strong card. Paint it a light color — this will let the collage objects placed on it really stand out. Choose some interesting things, such as shells, beads, or buttons.

2 Cover the frame with a thick layer of glue and position the objects. When dry, you could paint around the objects with silver paint, using a fine paintbrush. Put colored card behind the frame and display some of your favorite objects in the middle.

## COLLAGE WINDOW

Rough out a design on paper before you start making this project. Experiment to see which colors look best overlapping each other.

*1* Draw a decorative frame shape on card. Cut it out and use it as a template to cut another one the same size. Cut the plain acetate the same shape as the outside of the decorative frame.

*2* Paint both frames on one side. Glue the plain sides and sandwich them together with the clear acetate sheet in between. When dry, glue colored acetate shapes onto the clear acetate background.

*3* Use a hole punch to make a hole in the top of the frame, well away from the edge. Loop silver thread through here and hang the frame up in a sunny window.

▶ *The frame looks best if it is painted a dark color. If you like, decorate it with a silver pen or stick silver foil shapes onto it.*

# Toy-making

CHILDREN HAVE PLAYED WITH TOYS since ancient times and some of the oldest examples are still popular today. Using simple methods and everyday materials, you can make some of these traditional playthings.

## ROCKING HORSE AND RIDER

Here is an easy way to make a working miniature rocking horse. Once you have made this one work, try other animal shapes.

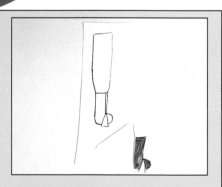

◀ *The rider sits on the matchbox, her legs over the side of the horse. Try designing your own shapes using this matchbox method. You could try a boat shape, or a rocking clown!*

**1** *Draw a rocking-horse shape on some card. Cut it out and then use it as a template to cut out another shape the same size. Lay the horse templates on a table, pointing opposite ways. Paint the side that you see.*

**2** *Stick the empty matchbox (without the tray) against the middle of one plain side of the horse and then, matching up the outlines, to the middle of the other plain side. Cut out a rider through two layers of a folded piece of card, as shown.*

**3** *Leave the top of the rider uncut at the fold. Paint it, cut out some legs from card, and then paint them. Fold each leg, as shown above, and stick them to either side of the body. Place the rider on the rocking horse.*

## COTTON-REEL TANK

Here's a version of the traditional moving cotton reel tank.

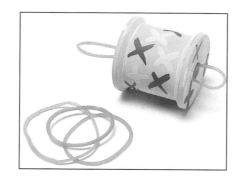

### WHAT YOU NEED

Card

Empty wooden cotton reel, painted brightly

Rubber band

Small candle (ask an adult to cut it into 0.75in (2cm) tablets for you)

Two dead matchsticks (ask an adult to cut the head off)

1 Pull the wick out of one of the candle tablets. Poke the rubber band through the hole in the middle (you may need to make this bigger with a sharp pencil). Make a straight groove across the top of the candle tablet.

2 Put a matchstick through the rubber band at one end of the candle and fit the stick into the groove. Push the other side of the rubber band through the hole in the cotton reel and loop it through the other matchstick so the stick lies flat against the cotton reel. The rubber band should now be held in place by the two matchsticks.

3 Wind up the matchstick on the candle end. Then put the reel on a flat surface, let go and see what happens!

Make lots of tanks, paint them in different colors, and organize races with your friends.

# Wobbling paper toys

Here is an easy way to make some toys that wobble from side to side. These ones are made from paper, but you could also use scraps of brightly-colored fabric.

◀ *You could make other simple shapes using this method. Try a dragon or a caterpillar.*

## Paper snake

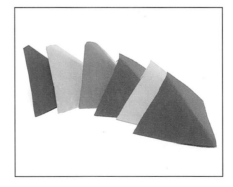

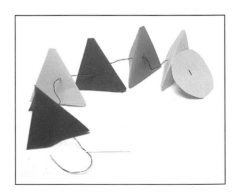

1 *Draw a diamond shape on the paper. Cut it out and use it as a template to draw lots of others, and cut these out, too. You can speed up this process by cutting through more than one paper layer at the same time. Then, carefully fold each paper diamond in half.*

2 *Thread the needle with a piece of string about 8in (20cm) long and knot it at the bottom. Push the needle through the tips of the folded diamonds. When you have 6in (15cm) of string full of paper diamonds, thread the needle through the bottom of the card cup.*

3 *Paint a face on the cup. Make two more lengths and tie them onto the first one to make arms and legs. Thread on cups to make hands and feet. If you like, finish each length with a circle of card before you put the cup on.*

Use an egg box cup for a head.

◀ *Make the body parts stiff by threading as much paper as you can on the string. Hang your doll up by a loop of thread.*

The bigger the diamonds, the fatter your doll will be.

71

# Clay jewelry

For centuries, potters have used clay to create works of art. You can do the same using self-hardening clay that does not need to be fired in a kiln. You can then paint and varnish your work to make beautiful things, such as necklaces, bracelets, and badges.

## WHAT YOU NEED

Self-hardening clay

Poster paint and an old tray

Metal jewelry fixings or safety pins

Necklace or string

## IDEAL GIFTS

Jewelry is easy to make from clay. Make different shapes, such as animals and rainbows. Before the clay hardens, make holes in the shapes for earring fixings or necklace thongs. Or you could tape a safety pin to the back to make a badge.

## A POINT TO REMEMBER

Use bright paints to bring the jewelry to life. Add stripes, dots and animal faces.

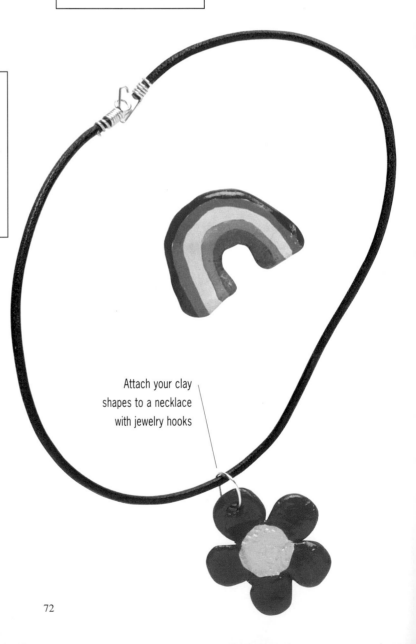

Attach your clay shapes to a necklace with jewelry hooks

These badges make great gifts.

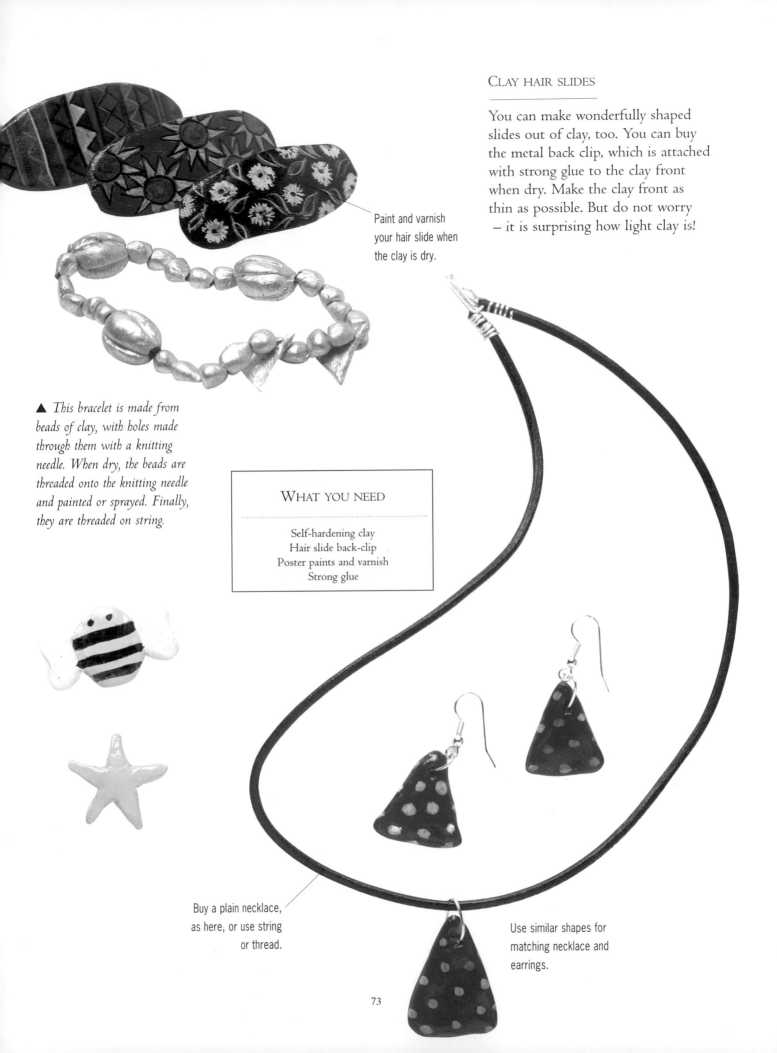

## CLAY HAIR SLIDES

You can make wonderfully shaped slides out of clay, too. You can buy the metal back clip, which is attached with strong glue to the clay front when dry. Make the clay front as thin as possible. But do not worry — it is surprising how light clay is!

Paint and varnish your hair slide when the clay is dry.

▲ *This bracelet is made from beads of clay, with holes made through them with a knitting needle. When dry, the beads are threaded onto the knitting needle and painted or sprayed. Finally, they are threaded on string.*

### WHAT YOU NEED

Self-hardening clay
Hair slide back-clip
Poster paints and varnish
Strong glue

Buy a plain necklace, as here, or use string or thread.

Use similar shapes for matching necklace and earrings.

73

# Clay crafts

THE BEST SURFACE TO WORK your clay on is a wooden board. You can get different textures on the surface by using the tools listed. If the clay starts to dry out and crack while you are working on it, wet your index finger and smooth over the crack.

## CANDLE HOLDER

Fit a candle into a spiral clay candle holder. It would look great on a dinner table.

*I Take a large ball of clay and two small balls. Roll the large ball into a long strip and wrap it round the base of the candle. Remove the candle. Make a bottom for the candle holder from another small clay disc.*

*2 Roll the two small balls into strips of clay. Twist them into a spiral shape. Wet the sides of the base and press the two spirals onto either side, as shown. When dry, paint the candle holder, then varnish it.*

*I Roll out long thin lengths of clay. Wind them in a spiral to form the base of the pot and then the sides.*

## MAKING A CLAY POT

It is possible to make lots of different-shaped pots out of self-hardening clay. Paint and varnish them. Then fill them with sweets or pot-pourri to make presents. The best way to begin pot-making is to start with a coil pot. Paint and varnish it when you have finished and the clay is dry.

*2 Join new lengths together with wet clay to continue the spiral up to the top. Press gently to make the pot firm.*

## MIRROR FRAME FROM SELF-HARDENING CLAY

Make a clay mirror frame and decorate it with stars and spirals, suns and moons, flowers, or letter shapes.

▶ *Paint the frame brightly and varnish it when the paint is dry. Tape a wool loop to the back so you can hang it up.*

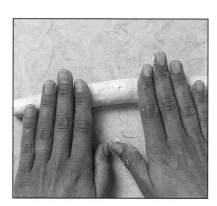

*1 Put a lump of clay on a clean surface such as a tray. Roll your hands over it as shown until it becomes a long evenly-shaped roll. Keep rolling it until it is long enough to go all the way round the edges of your mirror. It should be quite thick all round.*

*2 Carefully lay the roll round the edges of the mirror to form a rectangular frame. Join the roll ends by pushing them together, dabbing on some water and smoothing over the join. Push the roll down to fix it on and make it look flat.*

*3 Use clay tools or lolly and cocktail sticks to push different shapes and marks into the frame. Make clay shapes such as stars. Put small blobs of wet clay underneath them and push them onto the frame. Allow the finished piece to dry and harden.*

# Jewelry-making

THERE ARE LOTS OF DIFFERENT ways to make jewelry. Here are some suggestions to start you off. Once started, you can look in illustrated history books to get some inspiration for your own unique designs. People have been wearing jewelry since prehistoric times, so there are lots of style ideas to choose from!

## BEAD-MAKING

Painted clay beads look attractive strung on a necklace. You could make round beads, or try other shapes, such as flowers or pieces of fruit.

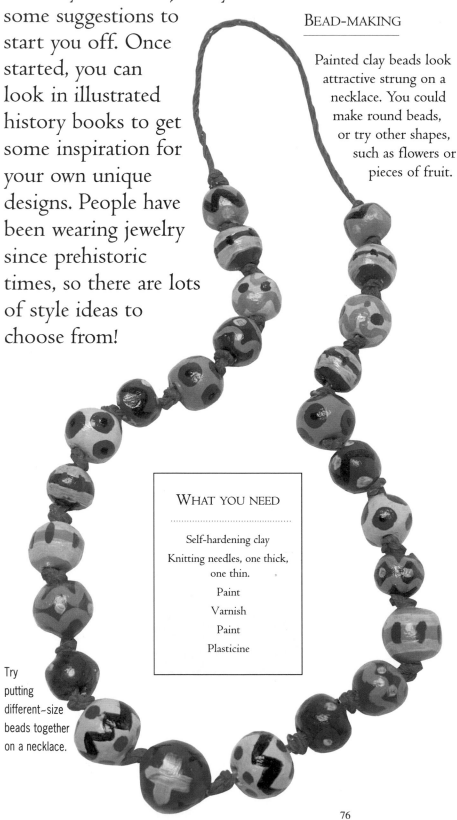

Try putting different-size beads together on a necklace.

### WHAT YOU NEED
..........................................

Self-hardening clay

Knitting needles, one thick, one thin.

Paint

Varnish

Paint

Plasticine

1 Roll the clay into balls and make a hole through each one with the thick knitting needle. Let them dry thoroughly.

2 Thread the beads onto the thin knitting needle so that they can turn easily. Rest the needle between two lumps of plasticine on newspaper. Paint the beads a plain color.

3 When the paint is dry, decorate the beads with colorful paints. When they are dry, varnish them. Leave them overnight before you use them in jewelry.

# NECKLACE

To thread a necklace, use something strong, such as plastic thread or thick embroidery thread. Either tie the two ends together or tie each thread tightly to a jewelry fixing. Before you start putting on decoration, make sure your thread is as long as you want it to be.

▶ *Buy a length of beaded thread from a dressmaking shop. Cut rectangles of different colored netting. Put a few layers together and tie them in a knot around the thread. As an alternative, you could tie on short lengths of colored ribbon instead.*

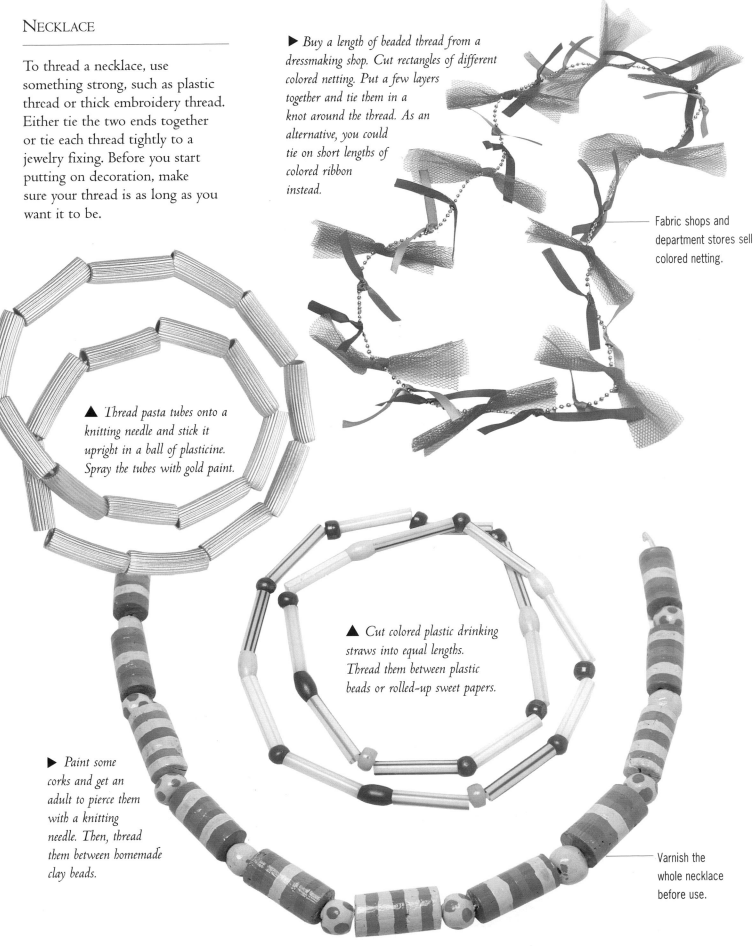

Fabric shops and department stores sell colored netting.

▲ *Thread pasta tubes onto a knitting needle and stick it upright in a ball of plasticine. Spray the tubes with gold paint.*

▲ *Cut colored plastic drinking straws into equal lengths. Thread them between plastic beads or rolled-up sweet papers.*

▶ *Paint some corks and get an adult to pierce them with a knitting needle. Then, thread them between homemade clay beads.*

Varnish the whole necklace before use.

77

# Bangles, brooches, and badges

Y OU CAN MAKE ALMOST ANYTHING into a badge or a brooch, or for the decoration on a bangle.

## BADGES AND BROOCHES

Start with a badge bar and glue a flat card shape onto it. Then glue objects onto the shape to make a brooch. Paint words, or glue pictures onto it to make a badge! There are some examples of this simple approach below.

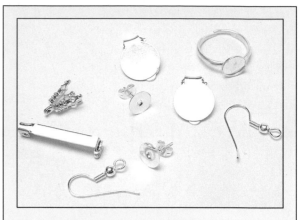

### JEWELRY FINDINGS

You can buy basic jewelry parts, called "findings," in craft shops. They cost very little and make jewelry-making a lot simpler. Get some strong glue to fix pieces onto the findings. Types of finding are shown above.

### WHAT YOU NEED FOR FAN BADGE

Scrap card

Paper fastener

Badge bar

Tape

Glue

Photos of your family, friends, or favorite stars.

▶ *Cut out four triangles. Decorate one side of each with a photo or message. Stick the badge bar to the back of one, well above the pointed tip. Lay the other triangles on top of the first one and use a pair of nail scissors to pierce a hole through all four near the tip. Put the paper fastener through this hole. Open it out and put sticky tape over the ends so they won't stick into you. Pin the badge on and then fan out the triangles.*

▶ *This badge is made from a jar screwtop. The edges act as a frame.*

◀ *This card circle is decorated with string and beads.*

## BANGLES

Make a plain bangle shape by cutting a ring from a clear plastic bottle, or making a ring of card.

▼ Decorate the card shape by sticking on beads and pieces of string to get an interesting raised pattern. Then spray over it with gold or silver.

▶ Decorate the plastic bottle shape by winding a fabric strip round and round it. Then glue the end of the fabric where it won't show.

◀ Make several lengths of plait from thick parcel string. Make a knot at the ends of each plait so some string tassels hang down. Stick each length around a black card bangle. Line up the knots and leave the tassels hanging down.

▼ This earring is made from two paper circles. Each circle was cut from the edge to the middle, then folded back and forth to make a fan. The circles were fanned out and then glued to a card circle, which was itself glued to an earring fixing.

## EARRINGS

The earring ideas shown here are glued onto a pierced ear or clip-on ear fixing.

◀ Bow wih thread sewn through the back of it. The thread hangs down. A bead has been threaded on each end.

◀ Small plastic toy.

# Puppet-making

**P**UPPETS HAVE BEEN MADE FOR MANY centuries. There are lots of different types, some simple and some very complicated and time-consuming. The easiest ones are finger puppets and glove puppets. The most complicated are many-stringed marionettes that move like real people!

## CONE PUPPETS

Use an A6 piece of scrap paper (a quarter of an A4 sheet). Lay your finger on it and roll the paper round it, rolling slightly at an angle to get a cone shape. Tape the tip of the paper down to keep the cone shape in place. Use felt-tip pens to color the cone. You could run a pipe-cleaner through the paper behind your finger.

▶ *To perform with finger puppets, crouch behind a table and wiggle your fingers above the edge.*

## FINGER PUPPETS

These are quick, easy to make, and very simple to work – you just use your own fingers!

## TUBE PUPPETS

Make a simple tube shape to fit your finger. One way to do this is to cut up the side of an empty toilet roll, cut a section out of it to make it narrower and then roll it up and tape it to fit your finger. Stick a card face on the front. For the very simplest finger puppet, just paint a face on the end of your finger and make a little paper hat, or use a thimble.

A card hat gives a puppet character.

Add a paper bow-tie and tape it round your finger.

Tie a ribbon or some embroidery thread around your finger to decorate a felt-tip face.

### WHAT YOU NEED

Scrap paper and sticky tape
Water-washable felt-tip pens

## GLOVE PUPPET

The simplest glove puppet is just a paper bag with holes for your little finger and thumb! The one shown below is made from felt. You can usually buy single squares of felt in craft or dressmaking shops. Design your puppet in a sketchbook first. Then you will know what color felt to buy and what else you need to collect.

The doll's hair is a clump of wool glued to the head and tied at the ends to make bunches.

Try stitching on buttons for eyes and gluing on a mouth.

Decorate the puppet's dress with strips of lace.

---

### WHAT YOU NEED

Two pieces of felt, both larger than your hand

Glue

Scissors

Pencil

Needle and embroidery thread

Pins

Buttons, braid, pieces of lace, etc, to decorate the puppet

Fabric pens or felt-tip pens

---

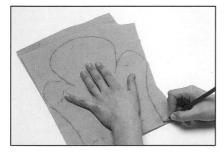

**1** *Lie the two pieces of felt together and pin them to hold them steady. Put your hand on the felt, with your thumb and little finger spread out. Draw a line 1.5in (4cm) outside the hand edge, running round the hand down to the straight edge of the felt. Carefully cut out both hand shapes.*

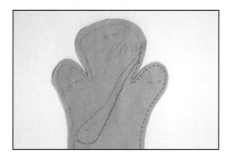

**2** *Put a line of pins 0.5in (1cm) inside the edge of the felt, leaving the bottom edge open. Draw a line if it helps. Sew along the line through both layers, doing plain running stitch, as shown above. Knot one end of the thread and oversew on the same spot a few times at one edge to strengthen the stitching.*

**3** *Glue or sew on felt shapes, buttons, and wool scraps to decorate the puppet. Draw on a face with felt-tip pens or fabric pens. To make a skirt, stitch loosely along one edge of a strip of scrap fabric. Pull both ends of the thread to gather up the material to fit round the puppet. Tie the ends of the threads at the back.*

# Recycled Ronnie

COLLECT BITS AND PIECES FROM YOUR kitchen to make this garbageman; then work him with a stick. Try making some friends for him, and write a play for them all to perform!

Yoghurt-pot hat, decorated with brown paper

## MAKING RECYCLED PUPPETS

Both these puppets are made from all kinds of things — old newspaper, card, empty yoghurt pots. Use anything you can find around your home!

▶ *To perform with Ronnie, position him above a table edge. If you want, make the table look like a garbage site, with rolled-up balls of paper and foil.*

Newspaper-strip fingers

### WHAT YOU NEED

Eight empty toilet-roll tubes

Old newspaper

Glue and sticky tape

Empty yoghurt pot

Two empty matchboxes or similar-sized cartons

Empty box, such as a teabag box

Eggshells, screw tops, etc, to decorate the puppet

Old sock and string

*1* *To make the head, push a ball of newspaper inside an old sock. Tie the bottom with string. Cut eyes, a nose, and a mouth from magazines, or use items, such as screwtops, to make a nose and eyes. Glue them on, with a decorated yoghurt pot for a hat.*

*2* *Roll up a 2in (5cm)-tube of newspaper and pull the sock neck down through it. Tape the sock in place. Cut a hole in the top of the body box and push the newspaper tube through, with some poking out for a neck. Tape the tube inside the box.*

*3* *To make arms and legs, place two toilet-roll tubes end to end, and tape them together inside one edge to make a hinge. Tape two of these tube-pairs to the bottom of the body, with the knee hinges at the front. Tape a tube-pair either side of the body to make arms.*

*4* *Glue empty matchboxes onto the legs for feet. Glue some newspaper rolls to the arms for hands. Cut them with scissors to make ragged fingers. Decorate Ronnie with string, scraps of newspaper, and lettering cut out from magazines. Tape or glue a stick up Ronnie's back to make him into a puppet.*

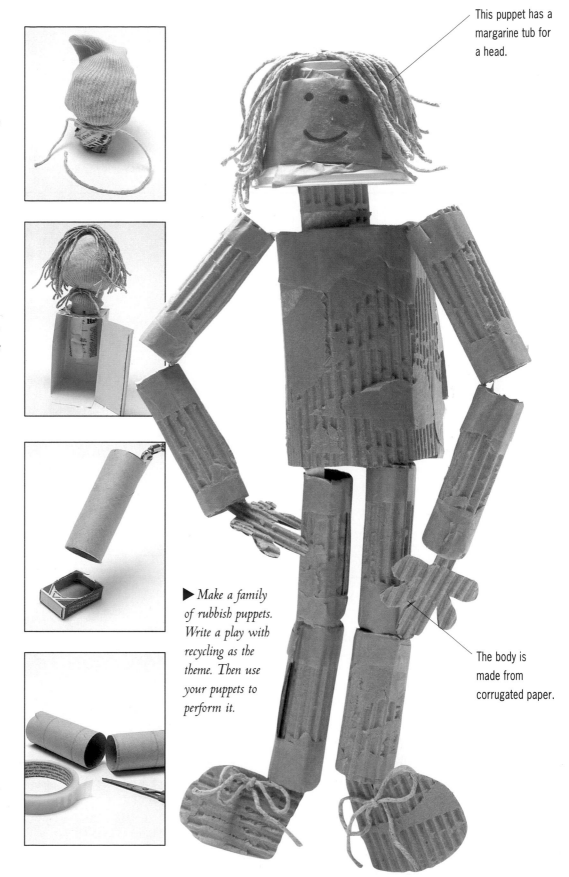

This puppet has a margarine tub for a head.

▶ *Make a family of rubbish puppets. Write a play with recycling as the theme. Then use your puppets to perform it.*

The body is made from corrugated paper.

# Birthday Crafts

For a special birthday, make some personalized costumes and a card that has hidden surprises! Show you really care, too, by making a birthday gift using any of the ideas from the pages of this book.

## WHEEL BIRTHDAY CARD

This card is simple to make and fun to receive.

### WHAT YOU NEED

A card square, 8in (20cm) x 8in (20cm)

A card rectangle, 8in (20cm) x 12in (30cm)

Compass and pencil

Scissors

Glue

Crayons, felt-tips, or paper scraps

Ruler

Paper fastener

1 Use a ruler to find the middle of the square. Draw a circle, using a compass set at 3in (8cm). Cut out the circle.

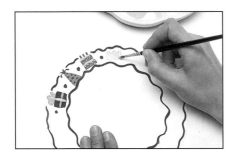

2 Decorate the edge of the circle. Write birthday messages and draw colorful pictures on a party theme.

3 Make a hole through the middle of the circle, using sharp scissors.

4 Fold the rectangle in half, as shown. Match the edges at the top. Press down lightly on the fold with your finger.

5 Cut a wavy line along the top edge of the folded rectangle.

6 Decorate one side with cut-out paper shapes. Open the rectangle and run a thin line of glue along the inside edges.

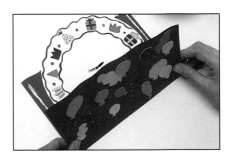

7 Push the paper fastener through one side of the rectangle and through the circle, as shown. Glue the sides together.

# BIRTHDAY HATS

**1** Use a compass to draw a circle with a diameter of 12in (30cm) on colored card.

**2** Cut out the circle carefully.

**3** Cut a line into the middle. Make a hole in the middle as shown.

**4** Cut into a piece of crepe paper 5in (12.5cm) x 2in (5cm) to make a fringe.

**5** Twist round the top of the fringed piece as shown.

**6** Stick the twisted piece into the hole in the circle. Tape it in, if you like.

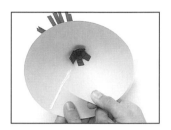

**7** Fold the card round to make a cone shape that will fit your head.

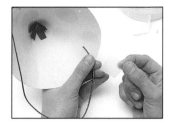

**8** Tape the cone in place. Tape on a piece of elastic to make a chin-strap.

**9** Stick cut-out colored shapes onto the cone to decorate it.

**10** Curl the fringe by running the strips along a scissor blade.

## PARTY CHAIN

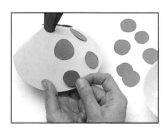

**1** Fold some crepe paper over and under as shown above.

**2** Draw a shape on the folded paper so it runs off each side.

**3** Cut out the shape. Then open the paper up to get a chain.

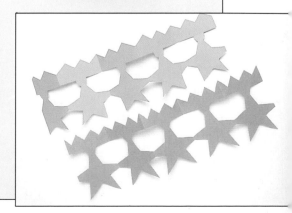

# Christmas crafts

CHRISTMAS WILL BE EXTRA-special if you make some decorations of your own. Try these easy ideas, and then flick through the pages of the book to get further inspiration. If you hold a different kind of yearly festival, adapt the Christmas theme to fit your own celebrations.

## CHRISTMAS CHAINS

Here are some ideas for making unusual tree decorations.

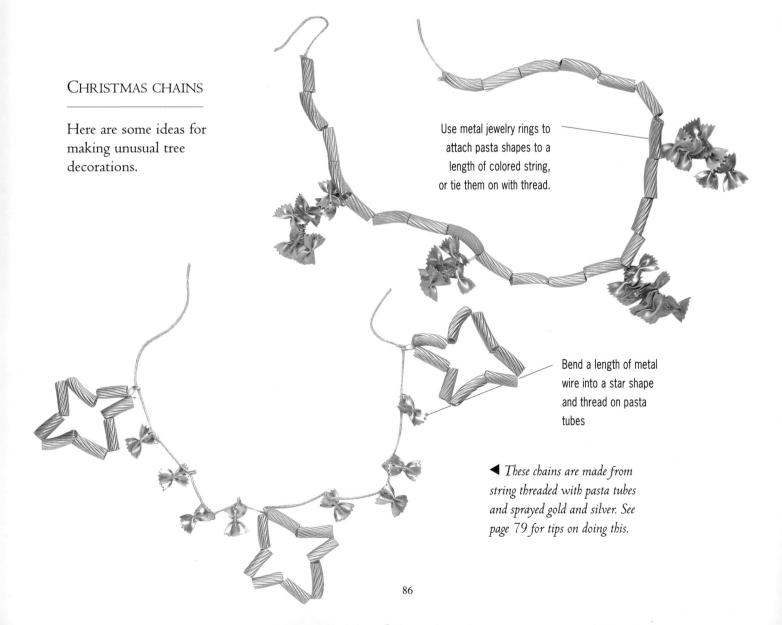

Use metal jewelry rings to attach pasta shapes to a length of colored string, or tie them on with thread.

Bend a length of metal wire into a star shape and thread on pasta tubes

◄ *These chains are made from string threaded with pasta tubes and sprayed gold and silver. See page 79 for tips on doing this.*

86

# PRETTY PRESENTS

Use colored netting to make
impressive present bows.

### WHAT YOU NEED

Netting

A needle and thread

4in (12cm) of thin ribbon, gold
thread or string folded
in half to make a loop.

Glue and foil

Scrunch some foil into a
sausage-shape and cover it
with netting to make a
decorative cracker.

# HANGING MOONS

These moons are easy to
make and look great
hung in a window.

### WHAT YOU NEED

A clean foil dish or
container

Scissors

Thread

*1 Flatten the foil dish, or
cut out the bottom.
Draw moon shapes on the
foil (the point of a pencil will
leave an incised mark).*

*2 Cut the shapes out of the
bottom of the dish. With
a scissor point, press gently
all round the shape of the
edge of the moon to make a
pattern, as shown.*

*3 Make patterns on both
sides of the foil using a
pencil point, as shown. Make
a hole in the top of the moon
and push through a loop of
thread to hang the mobile.*

# Present-wrapping

ERE ARE SOME EASY WAYS TO WRAP
and decorate presents so they look
almost too good to open!

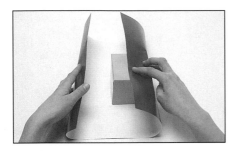

1 To cover a square-shaped box, wrap a larger piece of paper round it so that an edge hangs over either end. These edges should measure about half the length of the box. Secure the paper with sticky tape.

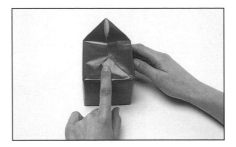

2 Fold both side edges into the middle in turn, creasing the paper to make them lie flat. The top and bottom edges are now triangle-shaped. Bring them together to meet in the middle, and tape them.

1 To cover an oblong-shaped box, fold the paper round it, with an edge hanging over either side. These edges should be as wide as the depth of the box. Tape the paper in place along the box.

2 Fold down a top edge so it lies flat. Then, fold in two side edges, creasing the paper so it lies flat. Fold up the bottom edge and turn over the pointed tip to make it neat. Tape it in place.

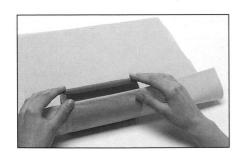

1 To wrap a present inside a pretty cracker shape, put the gift inside a cardboard tube. Wrap paper round the tube with the edges hanging over about 4.5in (12cm) at both ends.

2 Tape the paper to secure it round the tube. Then, twist the ends and tie them with ribbon, bunching up the wrapping paper. Snip the ends of the cracker into a fringe, or a zigzag line.

Crepe paper makes good wrapping paper since it is light and easy to fol

These printing blocks can be used to make the colorful wrapping paper, shown below

## WHAT YOU NEED

A square of card
6.5in (14cm) x 6.5in (14cm)

Two card rectangles
6.5in (14cm) x 4.5in (10cm)

Compass and pencil

Scissors

Glue

Crayons, felt-tip pens, or paper scraps
to decorate the card

Ruler

Paper fastener

## PERSONALIZED PAPER

To make your own unique wrapping paper, buy some plain-colored sheets. Then, cut out some squares of card for printing blocks. Stick string on the card in shapes, such as flowers, fish or hearts. When dry, dab poster paint onto the string and press them down firmly over the wrapping paper. You will need to keep adding more paint so that each printed shape is bright and sharp.

Add two or more printed shapes to one piece of paper.

89

# PRINT MAKING

## ELISABETH HARDEN

# CONTENTS

## Print Making

## Papercraft

# Introduction

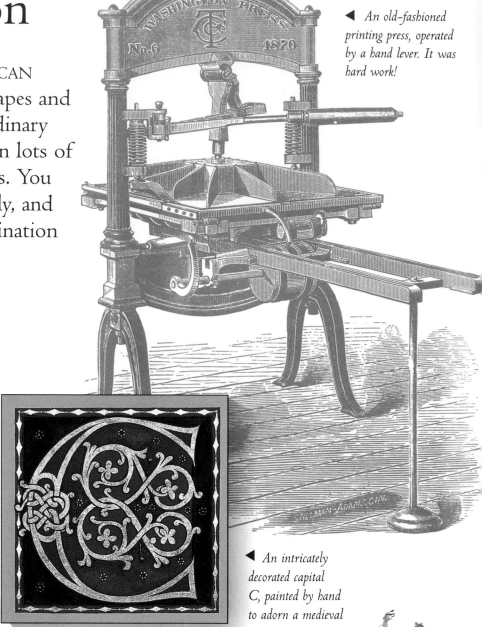

PRINTING IS FUN. YOU CAN make extraordinary shapes and textures from the most ordinary things, and repeat a pattern lots of times within a few minutes. You can decorate boldly, quickly, and cheaply, and let your imagination run riot to make beautiful pictures.

◀ *An old-fashioned printing press, operated by a hand lever. It was hard work!*

## THE PRINTING PRESS

This book would not exist without the invention of the printing press. This machine reproduces text repeatedly by pressing the ink from movable letter molds, called typefaces. Before this, manuscripts (meaning "written by hand") were made individually. Only the very rich could afford them. Print was one of the most important inventions in history, because it made the knowledge contained in books available to millions of ordinary people. Now it is all done by computers, and it's faster still!

◀ *An intricately decorated capital C, painted by hand to adorn a medieval manuscript.*

▲ *Here are the prints made by two different kinds of bike tires.* ▼

▲ *A paw print from your pet might look like this!*

## BASIC PRINTING

Any repeated pattern made by pressing something down onto a surface, or rolling it along, so that marks come off it over and over again, is printing. You've probably done it by accident lots of times!

▶ *Here's what happens if you walk on a clean floor with your muddy trainers . . .*

◀ *. . . or roll a dirty football around in the backyard!*

▼ *Rubber tires come in lots of interesting patterns.*

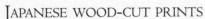

## JAPANESE WOOD-CUT PRINTS

Some of the very best prints were made in Japan in the 18th and 19th centuries. Japanese artists were inspired by the landscape — particularly mountains and oceans. Hokusai, who produced this mountain scene, is the most famous. He often used as many as 90 separate wood blocks to make his highly colorful, detailed prints.

# Materials and methods

HERE ARE SOME OF THE THINGS you will need to make prints. Most materials are very simple and cheap. The most useful of all is a box full of bits and pieces, scraps, and oddments which you can use to make wonderful shapes and textures. You will find lots of suggestions throughout the book. Printing can be a messy business, so it is important to have a large clear surface, plenty of newspaper, rags, and overalls. Then, with a few paints and some paper, you are ready to start!

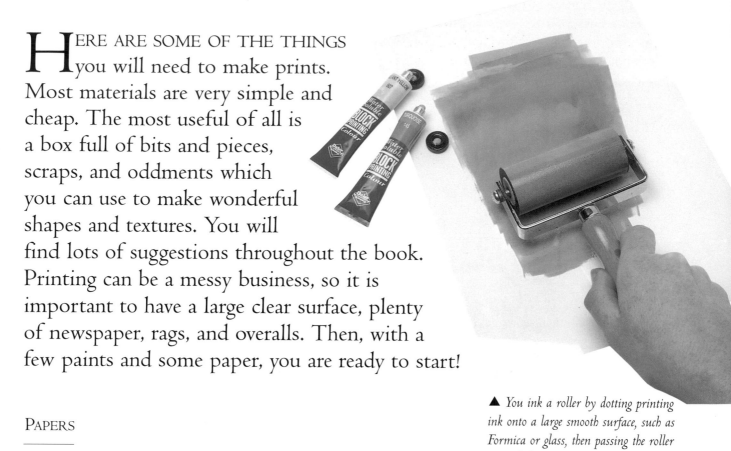

▲ *You ink a roller by dotting printing ink onto a large smooth surface, such as Formica or glass, then passing the roller up and down a few times. This transfers the ink to the roller, which you can then roll quickly over a sheet of paper.*

## PAPERS

As well as newspaper, which is a must, it is worth collecting different kinds of paper to experiment with. Drawing paper is essential, but blotting paper, tissue paper, and wrapping paper are also good. Keep plenty of scrap paper to try things out, too.

Stencil paper

Blotting paper

Drawing paper

Corrugated cardboard

Wrapping paper

Card

Lino

## PRINTING TOOLS

You will need a paint brush, glue brush, and toothbrush (for spattering paint). Some of the prints in this book were made by brushing paint directly onto a printing block, some by using other things like sponges or cardboard to make the marks. Other prints were made using a roller and an inked slab. This method gives a smoother layer of paint and is very easy.

Brushes

Pencils

Felt tips

Sponges

Scissors

Craft knife

Roller

## BURNISHING

To make a really clear print, you need to press the ink evenly right into the paper. This can be done with the back of a wooden spoon and is called burnishing. You could also use a clean roller on top of a sheet of clean paper. All professional printmakers are very clean and tidy and have places for everything. They are also very good at clearing up! Look at page 91 for how to organise things, and tips for drying and storing your finished work.

Poster paint

P.V.A. adhesive

## PAINTS AND INKS

Poster paint, either on its own or diluted with water, is fine for some printing, and you can make a huge range of colors by mixing. Many of the prints in the book are made with water-based printing inks, which work well with a roller. Some methods — such as marbling, screen printing, and fabric printing — require special inks and these will be described later.

Water-based printing inks

### SAFETY NOTE

You will be using things that need handling with care. Paints are messy, bleach can do damage, and blades and sharp points can hurt you. So be very, very careful, and keep a few sticking plasters nearby.

97

# Printing myself

YOU HAVE READY-MADE printing equipment at your fingertips – literally! A fingerprint is your very own mark: no one else has exactly the same pattern of whorls and circles. Many crimes are solved through police discovering tell-tale fingerprints, and footprints sometimes give the game away as well. There are other parts of the body that print in distinctive ways and make interesting patterns, too.

## FINGERPRINTS

Roll a thin film of printing ink onto a slab. Get your friends to press their fingers and thumbs in the ink and then onto a sheet of paper. If you look at these prints through a magnifying glass you will see that no two are the same.

It's easy to recognize a whole hand, but what about other parts? These creatures are made using fingers and thumbs. You could also experiment with knuckles, fingernails, even hair!

## FINGERPRINT BEES

With a few lines added, a fingerprint can become many different creatures. Try a swarm of bees that start as very small dots, then print with your fingertips to make them bigger. Add wings and features with a pen or pencil, then give them a beehive! Try drawing faces on a few prints and see what appears.

## SHOE PRINTS

Look at the soles of your shoes and see if they have a pattern. Many have ridges and ripples for particular reasons – gripping the ground on a sports field, preventing slipping in icy weather, walking on different surfaces, or just for decoration. How many shoe patterns can you find around the house?

Wrapping paper covered with lip prints.

## LIP PRINTS

Lips make wonderful prints. Put on a good thick layer of lipstick – it helps to look in a mirror to get a good shape. Now press your lips firmly onto a sheet of paper. Try making a kiss or a smile and see what happens.

A lip-print Valentine's Day card.

99

# Potato butterflies

Making marks by stamping an inked surface onto another surface is called relief printing. One of the easiest ways to make a relief print is to press an inked potato shape onto paper. You may have tried this already, and discovered patterns you can make with other simple vegetables. Use a big, even-shaped potato and start by cutting it neatly in half. Let the cut surface dry for about five minutes before you start.

## WHAT YOU NEED

Large potato or swede
Paint
Sponge
Saucers and plates
Thick paint brushes
Kitchen knife and craft knife
Pastry or cookie cutter
Plain paper and newspaper

## SIMPLE POTATO PRINTS

Using a craft knife, cut a design into the flat surface of one half of a good-sized potato – you could draw it beforehand with a felt-tip pen. Make sure that the potato outside the design is cut well away so that the edges will print cleanly. With a little practice, you can cut more complicated shapes, or you can use a pastry cutter for a ready-made design.

Now lay a piece of flat sponge in a saucer and cover it with paint, allowing it to soak in well. Press the potato block onto this printing pad, and then press it firmly onto a sheet of paper. When you have made several prints, the image will become fainter. Re-ink the block when you need to and then start again.

## BETTER PRINTS

- Place newspaper underneath the printing paper.
- Rock the potato slightly so that you make sure that all parts touch the paper.

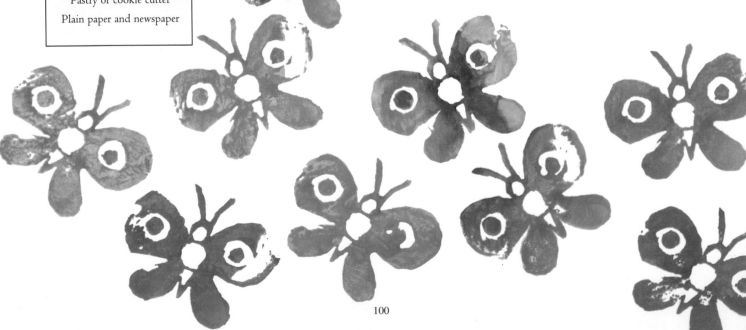

100

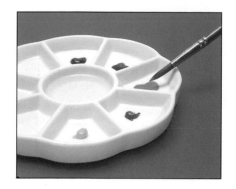

## MULTICOLORED BUTTERFLIES

Using different colors on the same block can sometimes produce exciting results. Mix puddles of thick paint in several colors on a palette, or a large plate. Paint these evenly onto different areas of the potato block. Press the block firmly onto the paper.

## ANOTHER BUTTERFLY

If you have any paint left, you can make another kind of butterfly. Fold some paper in half and open it out again. Paint some thick blobs of different-colored paint on one side, edging in to the fold mark. Fold the paper again, press it all over evenly, starting from the fold, open it carefully, and — hey presto!

Potato blocks don't last very long. If you want to continue printing later or change the image, slice off the old design and start again on the fresh surface. Other root vegetables, such as the swede or turnip, can make good printing blocks — try them and see which works best.

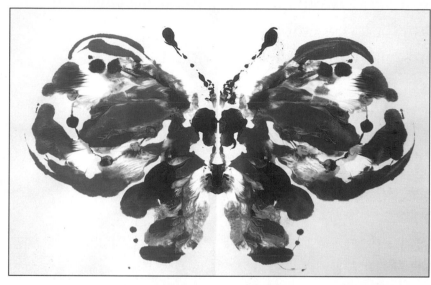

Repeat printing makes paler colors, overlapping blends colors.

◀ *Cutting the block in half down the center of the image will give you a different shape. These resting butterflies are made by cutting the first printing block in half.*

# Fruit and vegetable prints

Many fruits and vegetables have patterns of their own, and make wonderful ready-made printing blocks. Artists and designers have used these natural patterns to give them ideas for creating materials such as fabric and wallpapers. Try printing with as many fruits and vegetables as you can find and cut them in different directions. You will have some amazing surprises – and probably a few soggy messes!

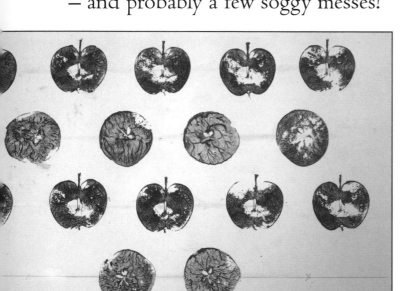

### PRINTS AND PATTERNS USING AN APPLE

Choose two firm apples, and cut one in half across the middle and the other from top to bottom. If you can find one with a stalk, the pattern will be more interesting. You can either press the fruit onto an inked sponge, or use a roller and printing ink. Take the crosswise-cut apple and press it into the paint or roll it all over with a roller, then press it onto some paper. Now try with the other apple – don't forget the stalk! Can you see the difference between the two prints?

### APPLE PAPER

To make regular patterned wrapping paper, draw guidelines over the page with a soft pencil and a ruler. Space dots evenly along the first line, and stagger them on the next line. Print apple prints on the dots. When dry, rub away the pencil marks.

Experiment with fruit and vegetable prints in odd colors.

Canopy of stiff paper
painted with colored stripes.

## Making a Greengrocer's stall

Here is a chance to show all your prints together. This greengrocer's stall has boxes of fruit in different colors. You could add your own name and advertising on the top.

### What you need

A selection of fruit and vegetables — for example, apple, pear, mushroom, cabbage, carrot, potato

Knife and scissors

Paint

Stiff white paper

Felt-tip pens

Brushes, or sponge printing pad

Grapes hang on
paper ropes.

Rolled-up tubes
for support.

Old shoe boxes, or box
shapes cut from white card,
display the produce.

Prints of apples, potatoes,
and cabbage fill the boxes.

# Trying other materials

Y OU CAN MAKE LONGER-
lasting printing blocks by
gluing objects to thick card. This is
called collage, from the French word
meaning "to glue." It's a chance to
be really inventive and to experiment
with lots of different materials and
textures. When you arrange the
items on the block, remember that
to print well they all need to be at
about the same level.

## WHAT PRINTS WELL?

Paper clips, sandpaper, materials such
as lace, buttons, small beads, crumpled
sweet papers, chains, dried peas and
lentils, rice, pasta.

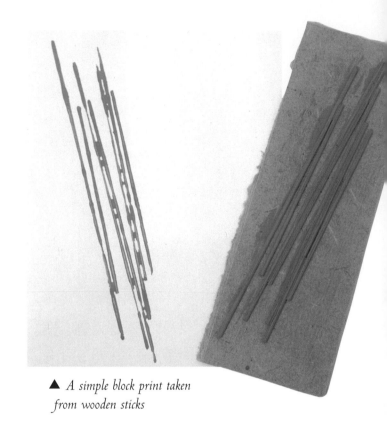

▲ *A simple block print taken
from wooden sticks*

## PRINTING WITH A PAPER DOILY

Lace-effects and frills can
be created quickly
and easily using
paper doilies.

Let the paint dry before you
lift the doily from the paper

## MAKING A COLLAGE BLOCK

Arrange materials that might print in an interesting way. Remember that the block will print better if the surface is level.

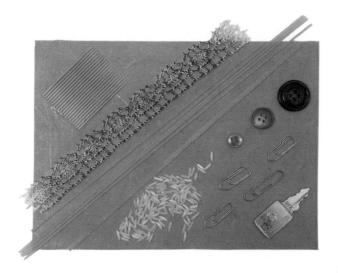

The block print would make a good book cover.

### WHAT YOU NEED

Materials to print

Cardboard or hardboard

PVA glue and glue brush

Printing ink or paint

Inking roller or paintbrush

Soft, thin paper for printing

I Cut a base of strong cardboard or hardboard, and spread it with a layer of glue. Press your materials firmly into the glue. Put a weight on top of the block and let it dry. Paint on a second thin layer of glue.

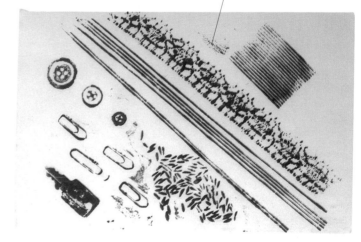

2 Cover your roller with ink and roll it evenly over your block. Place a sheet of paper over the inked block, hold it firmly with one hand, and press it down evenly all over with the other hand, with the back of a spoon, or with a clean, hard roller.

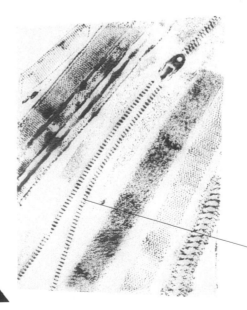

## A GLUE BLOCK

You can use glue itself to print. Spread it thickly over some card, and make patterns in it as it dries – you can press small objects into the surface, or create ripples by swirling a comb across it. When the block is dry, print it in the same way as the collage block.

Tapes and ribbons make great textures. The zip makes a railroad track!

## PRINTING A STRONGER IMAGE

If you use more pressure to print, you get a stronger picture. The traditional way of increasing pressure is to use a printing press, but you can use heavy weights – such as a garden roller, a mangle, or a large board covered with bricks or stones.

# Plain or stripy

THINK BEFORE YOU THROW OLD boxes and wrapping paper into the bin. Some of these materials are perfect ready-made printing blocks, and, with a little experimental cutting and tearing, you can print wonderful pictures from them. Corrugated cardboard has a ridged surface, so all the pattern-making is done for you, but you can cut and arrange it to make more complicated designs.

---

### WHAT YOU NEED

Smooth cardboard cut in the shape of sails

Pieces of thick card

Paint and inking roller or paint brush

Sponge and cotton wool

Old toothbrush and blunt knife

---

## MAKING HANDLES FOR PRINTING BLOCKS

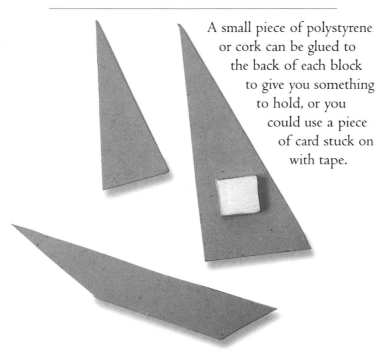

A small piece of polystyrene or cork can be glued to the back of each block to give you something to hold, or you could use a piece of card stuck on with tape.

## A GATHERING STORM

Printing blocks can be used again and again to create a range of different pictures. The same triangular shapes are used in the prints below to make boats on a calm sea as well as boats in a terrible storm!

1 *Paint a bright blue sky and a turquoise sea. Let it dry. Cut cardboard blocks in the shape of four sails of different sizes. Apply white paint with a roller or paintbrush, then press them onto the sea scene as if they were sailing in calm weather.*

2 *Now the wind is starting to blow and tipping the sails! The sky is painted grayer. The big clouds are printed with cotton wool, and the waves on the dark, churning sea are printed with triangles of ripped cardboard covered with white paint.*

## CUTTING CORRUGATED CARDBOARD COLLAGES

A mouthful of words, but what a mass of patterns can be made from one piece of corrugated cardboard! This print is made using blocks of corrugated paper, which have been arranged so that the lines run in different directions.

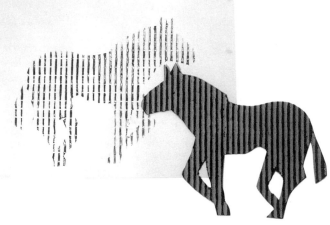

Rolls of corrugated cardboard, printed end on, make wheels, tank tyres, and cabbages. The cabbages at the far end of this field are made from smaller blocks, printed more faintly.

3 *The boats are blown right over in the gale! Dark gray clouds are printed with a sponge, and white spray is made by spattering paint from a toothbrush.*

▲ *Draw the shape of a zebra on the back of a sheet of corrugated cardboard. Cut out the shape, brush thick paint onto the ridges, lay your paper on top and press firmly to print.*

# Bits and pieces

Half the fun of printing is in finding the amazing marks left by quite ordinary objects. Sometimes these are obvious, but some are so strange that you can use them to make a guessing game to puzzle your friends.

It's hard to believe you could print from bubbles, but you can! Mix a little dishwashing liquid and water-based paint in a glass. Blow into the bottom through a straw until the bubbles reach the top of the glass. Lay a piece of paper gently over the colored bubbles, then peel it off with great care.

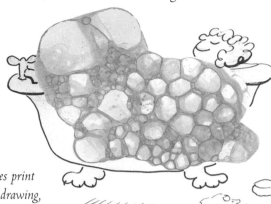

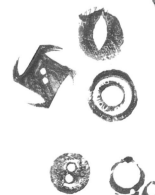

▶ *Try making your bubbles print into a picture by adding a drawing, such as this overflowing bathtub!*

## SET OF PUZZLE CARDS

These are some things you could try printing on cards to test your friends – a safety pin, a brush, a key, a fork, a doily, a length of tape. Look around your home to get more ideas. Try pieces of cork or wood, shells, bottle tops, bicycle tyres, and lengths of chain.

◀ *Try to spot which print comes from a sieve or a shoelace.*

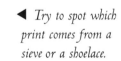

◀ *Prints taken from buttons can be used for decoration.*

## MAKE A MEAL OF IT

You'll find that you can make some prints that look exactly like things to eat. Try cutting out shapes and using the right colors to make platefuls of paper food! You can have lots of fun getting friends to try and guess what you made your printing blocks from. Can you work out how the baked beans on toast were made, without looking at the caption?

▶ *These prints were made from salad and vegetable leaves, potatoes, and apples.*

Tomatoes made from a cut apple

▲ *These baked beans are printed from bubble wrap and the toast from a sponge.*

◀ *The sausages are printed with fingers, an egg with a potato block, and bacon with scraps of ribbon.*

109

# Printing nature

NATURE HAS BEEN PRINTING ITS own image since time began. Perhaps you've seen the fossilized imprint of a delicate leaf or shell. Making a one-minute print from a leaf will leave a pattern that would take hours to paint with a brush! And remember, each side of a leaf will print a different pattern. A short treasure hunt outdoors could produce a whole collection of things to print – such as leaves, bark, seed pods, and twigs.

Corn stalks

## PRINTING LEAVES

Collect leaves with attractive patterns or strongly marked veins, in different shapes and sizes – skeleton leaves are very good. Seed pods and dried flowers have unusual textures. The more things you try, the more surprises you will have!

To take prints, roll some ink over the leaf, then lay your paper on top. Using a clean, dry roller, roll gently and evenly across the paper. Peel the leaf away from the bottom of the paper to see the wonderful pattern you have made.

Leaf prints

▶ *Leaves are delicate, so you need to take care when printing from them.*

Add insects to make a leaf print look like a tree!

## A FRIEZE OF LEAVES

Cover a long surface with newspaper and prepare your inks and rollers. Cut some lengths of lining paper approximately 3ft (1m) long and cut these in half lengthwise so that you have a long strip about 12in (30cm) wide. Lay this out on your surface and put a weight on each end. Lay some leaves on a sheet of newspaper and roll ink over them. Starting at one end of your paper roll, print a pattern of leaves. Use more than one color to make it more interesting.

▼ *You could join several friezes together to go round your room or the top of your bed.*

# Ferns, feathers, and fronds

SOME THINGS TAKE AN ENORMOUSLY LONG TIME to draw and paint, and are never quite as good as the real thing. By printing feathers and ferns, you can make an instant picture without all the fuss of tiny lines and thin brushes. With feathers, you'll need to collect quite a few because the fronds tend to stick together.

## BIRDS IN A BIRDBATH

Feathers make wonderful prints. Here, they are used to make birds splashing around in a birdbath and others in flight. The birdbath is cut out from paper sponged with gray paint and spattered with paint from a toothbrush. Draw the beaks and feet on later with a felt-tip pen.

Fern prints

## YOUR OWN CARRIER BAG

The easiest way to make a carrier bag is
to use a shop one as a pattern. Take it
to pieces along the joins, and cut your
own paper to the same shape. Or you
could glue your own paper onto an
existing bag, or – easiest of all – lay a
plain bag flat and print straight onto it.

### WHAT YOU NEED

Strong paper carrier bag

Large sheet of strong paper

Glue or sticky tape

Inks or paints

Thick string

Ferns or seaweed

Ink roller

Clean roller

Scissors, pencil, and ruler

1 *Use ferns to print black and
white patterns all over a large
sheet of strong brown paper. Each
side of a fern will give you a
different image.*

2 *When it is dry, cut out the bag
shape, and stick the sides together.
Tape string handles firmly to the
inside of the top edge – folding this
over first will make it stronger.*

Fern prints on a
carrier bag.

# Rubber stamping

RUBBER STAMPS ARE THE very best way of stamping images – they give clean, crisp edges, and take a long time to wear out. They are often used to stamp letters and passports and all kinds of documents. Rubber printing sets are quite cheap to buy, but it is more fun to make your own!

▲ *You can buy lovely ready-made rubber stamps like these with quite elaborate patterns. Use food coloring instead of ink, and you can stamp them (gently!) onto iced cookies, but do first make sure the coloring is safe to eat.*

## MAKING YOUR OWN

Draw a design on the flat surface of a large eraser with a felt-tip pen. Use a craft knife to cut away the rubber around the shape, making sure that you don't cut too much. Try to avoid cutting under your shape, because that will make it less firm. Try it out first on rough paper to see what kind of pattern it makes. You may need to neaten the edges or make the shape simpler. If you have a disaster, don't worry – just slice off the surface and start again!

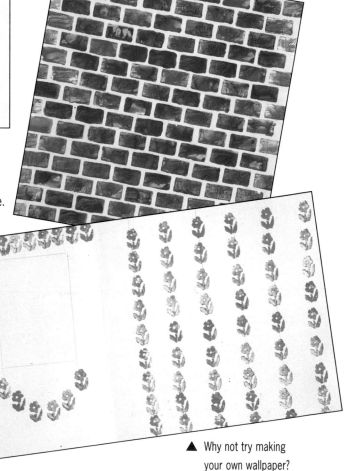

▶ This brick wall would be great for a dolls' house.

▲ Why not try making your own wallpaper?

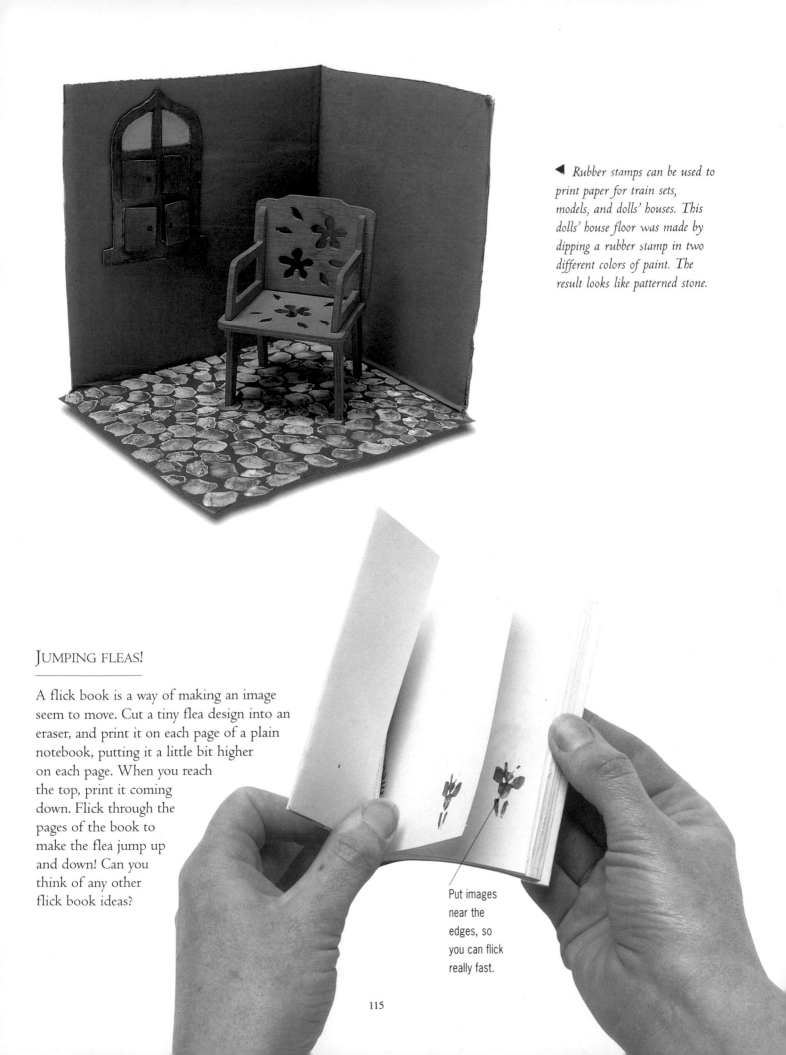

▶ *Rubber stamps can be used to print paper for train sets, models, and dolls' houses. This dolls' house floor was made by dipping a rubber stamp in two different colors of paint. The result looks like patterned stone.*

## JUMPING FLEAS!

A flick book is a way of making an image seem to move. Cut a tiny flea design into an eraser, and print it on each page of a plain notebook, putting it a little bit higher on each page. When you reach the top, print it coming down. Flick through the pages of the book to make the flea jump up and down! Can you think of any other flick book ideas?

Put images near the edges, so you can flick really fast.

# Animal footprints

Have you ever painted a really lovely picture, left it to dry, and found that your dog or cat has walked all over it, leaving muddy footprints? Or have you noticed a slab of newly laid concrete where a dog has left its pawprints? Prints left by animals are very distinctive, and can give you lots of information long after the animal has gone. They also make interesting patterns!

▲ *When marks like this cat's pawprints are made on top of the paper, the print is called positive. The shapes left inside something soft that has been dented, like snow or sand, are called negative prints, or imprints.*

◄ *People use animal imprints in many ways. Hunters sometimes follow game by tracking the marks that animals leave in wet ground, sand, or snow. Native Americans are very skilled at reading tracks. They can tell how many animals are in a group, how fast they are going, and even how long ago they passed.*

▲ *Making imprints with bare feet in the sand is always fun! Try to find smooth, firm sand that is just slightly damp.*

◄ *The horseshoe stamp made from this eraser prints on top of the paper, so it is positive.*

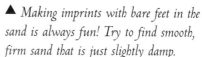

Cover a large box with brown paper, or leave it if there is no printing on it. Make blocks in the shape of different animal paws out of pieces of cardboard – here, we've made the marks of a penguin and a mouse Print them all over the surface, disappearing beneath the lid. Add others if you like. Then hide some toy animals inside!

Cut-out animals – and their footprints!

Mouse prints made with finger and thumb

Ant prints made with a rubber stamp

117

# Coiled string and wire

STRING IS EASY TO COLLECT. THERE are many different thicknesses and patterns of string, rope, and plastic-covered wire. You can make lots of interesting prints by winding and curling them, either just on their own or first made into a printing block.

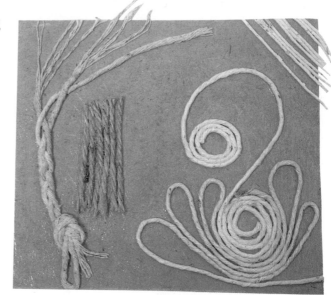

## A STRING BLOCK

First choose your string and get it ready — you can use lots of different kinds, or one long piece curled round and round. Cover a cardboard block with plenty of glue, wait until it is tacky, and lay your string on top. String can be springy so you may need to hold it in place. Put a weight on top of the block, and leave it to dry. Put several thick layers of wettish paint on the block — string is very absorbent. Lay a sheet of paper on top of the block, press all over evenly with your fingers or a clean roller, then peel the paper off.

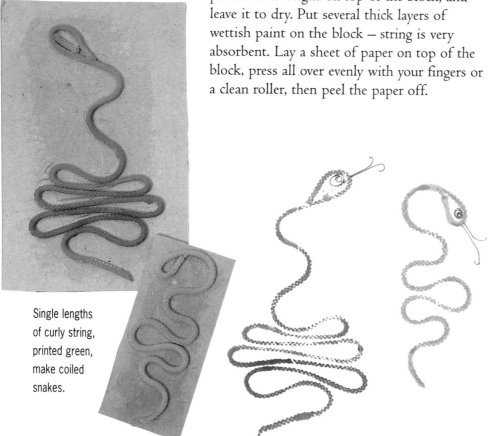

Single lengths of curly string, printed green, make coiled snakes.

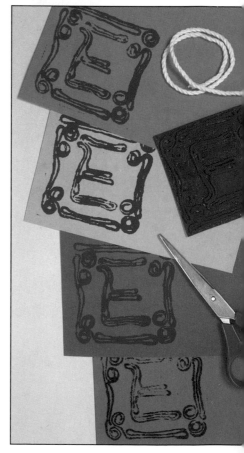

▲ *Pieces of string coiled tightly together make a decorative block to print your own initial. Remember to put on plenty of paint before printing.*

## PULLED STRING PRINTS

Fold a piece of paper in half, open it up, and smear some white chalk across the surface. Mix some pools of fairly thick paint and dip a piece of string in each until they are well coated. Lay the strings across the paper with the ends hanging out, and fold the paper again. Holding the paper firmly with one hand, pull the strings out with the other. Inside, you will have printed lovely swirly patterns.

## EDIBLE PATTERNS

Bend thick plastic-covered wire into a pattern and glue it onto a block of cardboard the same size as a piece of toast. Remember to write letters the wrong way round (the way they would look in a mirror), so that they will print the right way round. Press the block firmly into a thick slice of bread. Toast the bread, and your pattern will appear as if by magic!

# Printing landscapes

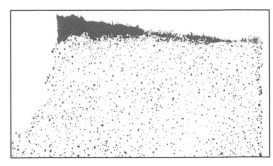

▲ *The rough texture of sandpaper makes excellent cliffs. Print with the rough side for the stony cliff face, and use the smooth side for the grassy clifftop.*

Now you've tried making printed marks with different things, start thinking up ideas about what kind of pictures you would like to print. Try a landscape – either find a real subject outside, or copy from a favorite picture. And, of course, you can always print something from your imagination – such as the Moon's surface or a primeval swamp!

## WHAT YOU NEED

Sandpaper, several grades
Cardboard
Paints
Printing inks
Roller
Glue
Celery stick

Add spikes on the cacti with the edge of a piece of card.

The hovering birds were made with a slice of celery.

Use a circle of card for the sun.

## GRAND CANYON

Draw a rough outline of your picture on a large sheet of paper, and fill in the sky and distant landscape with paints or crayons. Use paper covered with thick yellow paint to print the clifftop, and different-sized pieces of cardboard for the cliffs.

## MAKING THE MOST OF COLORED PAPER

Simple shapes of torn paper and card
make very effective printing blocks
when you use them on different-colored
background papers.

▲ Icebergs floating in a blue sea

▲ Misty mountains in a pale blue sky

▶ Rough rocks in yellow sand

▲ A cauliflower sprig makes a brilliant tree!

# Disappearing ink

I NSTEAD OF PRINTING COLOR ONTO the paper, you can start by inking the paper and then making the color disappear so that the white paper shows through. This is done with bleach, which can be dangerous so handle it with care and cover yourself up well. Don't let it touch your clothes or any furniture.

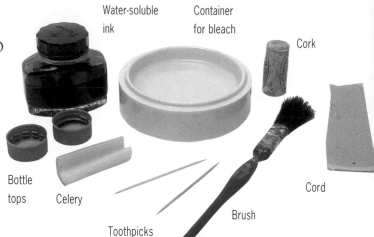

Water-soluble ink

Container for bleach

Cork

Bottle tops

Celery

Toothpicks

Brush

Cord

## PRINTING WITH BLEACH

Always cover your work surface with plenty of newspaper, and cover yourself with a big overall – bleach can do damage. Paint a layer of water-soluble ink all over a large sheet of paper. While it is drying, rough out a picture on paper – here it is a fish in the sea. You print or draw with bleach instead of paint, which makes the ink disappear.

The fish scales are printed with celery and a cork.

Make fine lines with a toothpick or twig, dipped in bleach.

The bubbles are printed with bottle tops and the end of a cardboard tube.

122

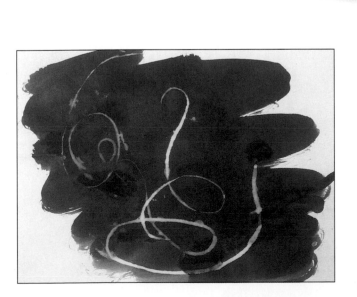

## MAKING A FRAME

Your pictures will look really good if you frame them. Cut a rectangle of white card so the inside edge is the right size to show your picture, and the outside edge is several inches larger. Paint the card with watered-down or soluble ink, and use bleach to print a pattern on it that matches your picture.

◄ *Experiment with using bleach to take out the colours of other inks and paints.*

### SAFETY NOTE

Don't let bleach touch your hands, eyes, or clothes. If it does, wash it off immediately with plenty of cold water.

# Marbled patterns

Marbling is an exciting process because you are never quite sure what kind of pattern is going to appear! It works because oil and water don't mix — the oil in the paint stays on the surface of the water, and will stick to the paper when you take a print. The swirly patterns make wonderful backgrounds to print on. Once you've started marbling you won't want to stop.

*1* Mix your paint in a pot with white spirit until it is runny. Half fill the tin with water. Swirl the paint around on the surface of the water using the end of your paintbrush.

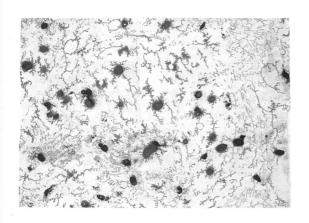

## WHAT YOU NEED

Oil paints, or powder paints mixed with cooking oil

White spirit

Paintbrushes

Old yoghurt pots

Old baking tin or tray

Newspaper

*2* Lay a sheet of paper very gently on the top of the water, and smooth away any bubbles. Take care not to push the paper under the surface.

*3* Lift the paper off gently from one end, and lay it flat to dry.

## BETTER MARBLING

Adding a little wallpaper paste to the water makes marbling easier to do.

## A GOLDFISH POND

The swirly patterns of marbled paper make a good "water" effect in a picture. Here, it's used for a fish pond, with color prints round the outside for the stone. Paint some orange goldfish in the pond with thick paint. Mix some green paint and paint a few lily leaves overlapping the fish. Then add a watchful cat!

*All these papers have been made by marbling. Use sheets of marbling to cover books or folders. With smaller scraps you can make or decorate cards, jewelry, or paper patchworks. You can even marble ribbon.*

# Backgrounds and distance

Y OU CAN HAVE FUN MAKING SKIES and backgrounds with printing. It is the best and quickest way to paint large areas very quickly. Also, it is very good for making clouds – especially dramatic storm clouds.

Different-sized cabbage leaves are very good for printing trees. Try other leaves as well for a range of effects.

## TREES IN THE PARK

A few cabbage leaves, printed onto white paper, then cut out, made nearly every tree in this park! Yellowy-green ink was rolled onto a slab and used for some of the trees. Then, blue ink was added to make mid-green, and more blue to print the darkest trees. The park fence was printed with the edge of a piece of card.

## DISTANCE EFFECTS

You can create the feeling of distance very easily with printing, by making things that are far away look faint. Look at the picture of the cabbage field and tractor on page 23. In the foreground, the cabbages are big and bold, and they get smaller and fainter in the distance. Practice controlling the amount of ink or paint that you transfer to the paper.

▶ *Alternating faint with strong color also makes lovely patterns. Here, three mushrooms were sliced in half to make printing blocks of different sizes, to correspond with the different strength of color.*

## SPONGING SKIES

Using a sponge is a kind of printing technique, as it involves transferring paint over and over again from the same "block." It is great for skies and clouds. Experiment with different colors, some printed on top of each other.

# Print the town

Whether you live in a city, town, or village, you can find exciting shapes and textures in buildings. Dramatic skylines cut from strips of card look wonderful as prints. Walls and roofs can be built up by printing a simple block again and again. The textures of brick and stone can be particularly interesting, so look around to see what you can create.

## Roofs

In many parts of the world, roofs are made from materials found locally.

Orangy red paint on cardboard shapes for Mediterranean rooftops.

To print a straw-roofed hut – use straw!

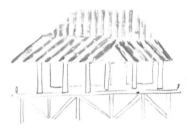

Blocks of corrugated cardboard for corrugated metal roofs.

## Sunset riverside

First paint a background of sunset and river. Then make a drawing in the shape of a city skyline on stiff card. With a sharp knife, cut out round the edges of the drawing. Use this card as a block, roll dark paint onto it and press it firmly onto the paper. Then wipe the block clean, and roll a thin layer of paler paint onto the other side. When you press this gently upside down, you've made an exact reflection of the skyline in the river.

## A WALL PINBOARD

Why not make your own fun pinboard to look like a wall?

Stick wrapping paper onto a pinboard to make a smooth surface (it need not be a single sheet). Make a card block in a brick shape and print a regular pattern over the whole area. Sponge on some gritty patterns to make the wall look rough. When it is dry, coat it with a thin layer of PVA to seal it. Let this dry.

### WHAT YOU NEED

Sheet of pinboard to cover

PVA

Paint

Paint brush

Wide glue brush

Card blocks

Sponge

Sandpaper

## BRICKWORK

If you want to have brickwork in a picture it is much quicker to print it than to paint it. First paint a background color, and then print blocks of color in a regular pattern.

*Brick textures can also be made by wrapping masking tape around a block of cardboard and using it to print.*

▲ *Use your pinboard for messages and your favorite photographs. You can write messages or scribble graffiti with a felt-tip pen or chalk — since the surface is sealed with PVA, you can wipe it clean again with a damp sponge. And you can add your own drawings — a mouse is living in this wall!*

# Fantastic flowers

Flowers are among the most popular and colorful things to print – they can be whatever you want, realistic or invented. Look around for ideas from dress or furnishing fabrics, and pretty wallpapers. You can even make printed flowers into a pretend bouquet!

▲ *A delicate stenciled tablecloth will enhance any vase of flowers.*

## CARDBOARD FLOWERS

These wonderful irises were made by printing with the edges of strips of cardboard.

▶ *Print some flowers, cut them out, and wrap them up in cellophane for a present!*

## A PRETTY BOUQUET

You can make bright flowers very easily by melting the wax from crayons. Take care with the hot iron!

▲ *Long strips were dipped in thick green paint, and pressed onto paper to make leaf shapes. Blue flowers were made with smaller strips, arranged in a fan shape to make the petals. Yellow and pink dots were added later.*

1 *Fold a piece of thick paper in half and open it out again. With a vegetable peeler, shave some pieces of wax crayon onto one side of the sheet.*

2 *Fold the paper with the wax inside, and iron over it very gently with a warm iron. The wax will melt into wonderful flower shapes.*

## FLOWER TEXTURES

You can get interesting effects by printing through textured material. These speckled petals were made using a piece of net.

## RUBBING CRAYON

Rubbing wax crayon gently onto paper with an eraser gives very delicate, smudgy colors.

▲ Draw flower shapes on stiff paper, and cut out the insides to make stencils. Color round the edges of the shapes with a wax crayon. Then lay the shapes on some drawing paper. With an eraser, rub the crayon color gently onto the paper beneath. The stencils will give clear edges to your flowers.

# Stenciling

Early settlers in North America could not afford imported wallpaper or decorated furniture. So they printed their own patterns with stencils. This is a wonderfully easy method of making a sharp, clear image – and you can use your stencil again and again. The secret of cutting a stencil is to leave a good width of paper (a "bridge") between the cut-out areas, so that the shapes stay separate when you've inked them.

▲ *You can get striking effects by using gold or silver paint, or stippling little dots of paint from a stiff brush instead of painting solid color.*

## A READY-MADE STENCIL

A paper doily makes a good stencil – lay it on a sheet of paper and sponge or brush paint through the holes.

---

### WHAT YOU NEED

Stencil paper or firm drawing paper

Sharp knife

Stencil brush

Pencil

Paints

Sponge

---

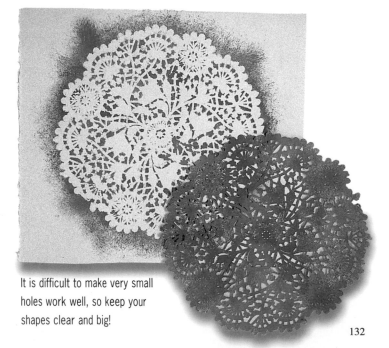

It is difficult to make very small holes work well, so keep your shapes clear and big!

## CUTTING A STENCIL

Always make a detailed drawing of your design first, keeping the shapes clear. Don't leave too narrow a strip of paper between the cut-out shapes – it might tear, or your ink or paint might run beneath it. Hold the stencil in place with masking tape at the corners or edges, so that it doesn't slip around.

# IDEAS FOR STENCILS

Stenciling is an ideal way to make borders – try one on an old box or some furniture. Or stencil a pattern on a plant pot, fix it with a coat of varnish, and give it as a present.

*1 Outline the shapes on your stencil paper, using a continuous line with no crossings.*

Light pencil guidelines will keep your borders straight – you can erase them afterwards.

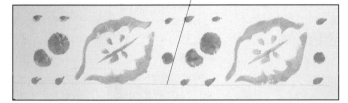

*2 Mix your paints, keeping them fairly dry. Sponge or paint color through the spaces.*

▲ *Fold a square piece of paper four times, then cut a stencil through all the layers. When you open it out, you'll have the same pattern in each section of the sheet.*

▼ *This wonderful multi-colored print was made using a number of stencils.*

▶ *This multi-colored picture has been made using a number of stencils.*

A sponge is good for larger areas.

Use a brush for the smaller shapes.

Make as many eggs as you like!

# My word!

STENCILING IS A VERY GOOD WAY of printing neat and tidy letters, which you can arrange into words to make big, bold labels for things. When you make a stencil alphabet, do not throw away the inside shapes of the letters – you can use these as printing blocks. That way you get two whole alphabets at the same time!

## ALPHABET STENCILS

You can buy a set of alphabet stencils very cheaply, but it's fun to make your own. Any strong card will do, but special stencil paper is better because you can wipe it clean and use it again and again.

**1** *Divide a sheet of card into equal sized squares, leaving a space between each square and between each row. Make enough squares for each letter or number you want to print.*

**2** *Draw a letter in each square. Make the shapes clear and solid so they will print boldly.*

**3** *With a craft knife, cut out each shape. This can be difficult, so take care or ask for help. Keep both the stencil letters and the cut-out letter shapes.*

# Decorated letters

Decorated letters look wonderful. If you cut an elaborate stencil containing decoration, you can use different colors for the different parts. These look really good on folders, boxes, and wrapping paper. Why not make a whole set of writing paper and cards with your own name or initials on?

Print these letters on posters, labels, and wrapping paper.

A decorated letter makes a very special book cover.

You can use letter stencils to make pictures, too!

Stenciled letters personalize this envelope.

# The four seasons

TREES CAN LOOK COMPLETELY DIFFERENT with each season of the year. You can use a range of printing methods to decorate one tree shape, to make it change from spring blossom to summer fruit, from fall leaves to bare winter branches. Then put all four together to give you a year-round picture.

Tree printing block

Apple print made from potato block

### TREES IN SEASON

Draw a bare tree on a sheet of stiff paper. Cut around the shape and either use the mask as a stencil or the tree as a printing block. Print the tree trunk four times, and decorate each one with images from a season of the year.

### SPRING

*Roll pale green paint onto some leaves and print them on the branches. Print round pink and white shapes for the blossom — you could use the end of a carrot.*

### SUMMER

*In summer the leaves are darker and apples grow on the branches. Print the leaves a deeper green, and make apples with a potato block dipped in red or green paint — or a mixture of the two.*

## WHAT YOU NEED

Cardboard

Craft knife, scissors, and glue

Four large sheets of paper

Leaves and carrots

Potato block

Felt-tip pens and brushes

Paints

Sponge

Glitter

Snowflake stencils

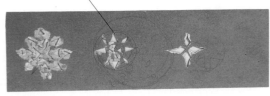

## FALL

*Trees in the fall are covered with rich golden leaves. Make an explosion of color with orange and red leaf shapes, and let some drop on the ground like golden coins.*

WHAT YOU NEED
.........................................
Paper the width
of your picture
Dowelling a little
wider than your picture
Glue and string

## WINTER

*Paint a darker background for winter, leaving the tree bare. Stencil white snowflakes in the sky. If you like, scatter some glitter on the paint while it is drying to make the snow sparkle.*

## HANGING PICTURES

Once you have made a series of pictures it's nice to display them in an attractive way.

1 *Stick a length of strong paper to the top of your picture, at the back, so that is sticks up about 6in (15cm). Fold this over to the back and stick just the edge down, leaving a tunnel along the top.*

2 *Cut out squares along the folded edge. Thread a piece of dowelling or thin bamboo through the tunnel, and hang it on the wall with string.*

137

# Cameras and computers

Photographers make their prints in a darkroom by shining a bright light through negative film onto special paper. Computer prints and photocopies are made by an even more complicated process. With these methods it is best to let science do the processing, and you can just have fun with the results.

## Snapshot collage

If you have a collection of snapshots or cuttings, you can display them for everyone to enjoy in a collage. Arrange some of your favorite things on a sheet of cardboard. When you're happy with the positions, stick each one down. Look at page 53 for how to make a hanging frame to put your collage on the wall.

## Computer art

Perhaps you have worked or played with a computer, and know some of the possibilities of these amazing machines to make extraordinary repeated patterns. If your computer has a color printer, so much the better!

## USING A PHOTOCOPIER

A photocopier is a quick way of making many copies of a picture. You can often make your picture larger or smaller, too.

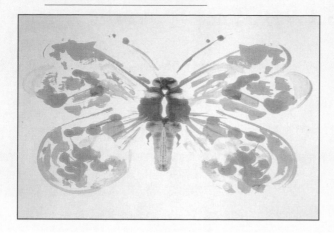

*Photocopiers don't just print from flat artwork or paper. This odd shape was made from a photocopy of a crumpled glove — with an eye, some whiskers, and rabbit teeth added!*

## PRINTING YOUR OWN T-SHIRT

You can print a photocopied picture onto any smooth fabric, such as a T-shirt, pillowcase, or bag. Like lots of printing methods, it will print your picture backwards, like that in a mirror. To get it the right way round, ask for a reverse photocopy to be made. This is most important if you have words or numbers in your image!

### WHAT YOU NEED

Photocopy transfer medium (available from craft shops)

Thick brush

T-shirt or fabric

Sponge

Photocopy of your picture

Clean roller

Foil or plastic sheet

1 *Lay the T-shirt on a flat surface and put a sheet of foil or plastic inside. Brush a layer of the transfer medium onto a photocopy of your picture, then lay it front side down on the fabric. Press firmly with a clean roller and leave to dry.*

2 *After a few hours, peel off the photocopy, and rub away the backing with a sponge. Your printed picture will appear! Paint another coat of the transfer medium on top of the picture and let this dry to seal the print.*

# Monoprints

A MONOPRINT IS UNLIKE ANY other print. Its name means "one print" and what you make can never be repeated. A monoprint is made by pressing a piece of paper onto an inked slab. The textures and shapes you can get are impossible to create by painting. They will be unpredictable – sometimes a mess, but sometimes brilliant!

## DESIGNING A COCKEREL

Many artists have used the cockerel as an inspiration for paintings or prints. Its proud stance and the texture and patterns of its feathers and skin make it very exciting to draw.

1 *Spread printing ink on a glass slab. Use brushes, twigs, and anything that makes an interesting mark to draw an image into the ink. Wipe areas of ink away with a rag. Work quickly and boldly until you have a design you like.*

2 *Lay a sheet of paper over your design. Holding it in position, use your hand or a clean roller to press the paper onto the paint. If you want to add more colors, fix one side of the paper to the slab with sticky tape. Fold the paper back to dry.*

3 *Add different-colored ink to the slab, and lay the paper back down to print again. The fixing tape makes sure it goes back in exactly the same position, which is called "registering."*

| WHAT YOU NEED |
| --- |
| Glass or Formica slab, or thick acetate sheet |
| Water-based printing inks |
| Paint brush |
| Paper |
| Clean roller |
| Rags |

### SAFETY NOTE

If you use a glass slab, make sure the edges are smooth or rounded.

## DRAWING A PRINT

Here is another way of making a monoprint.

Put colors on the slab in the areas you want them in the finished print.

1 Roll bands of two different colors of printing ink onto one slab at the same time. Place a sheet of fairly thin paper very lightly on top.

2 Draw a design carefully, pressing hard only where you draw. Lift the paper off and you'll see that the colors have printed your design in reverse, with lighter, smudgier colors in the background.

◀ Cover your books or folders with your best combed pattern prints. Try to place the most interesting patterns on the front.

▲ Roll bands of color onto the glass slab. Cut some cardboard combs, scrape patterns into the ink, then take a print. Sometimes the paints merge together and make other colors, sometimes they form thick ridges. The results are always unexpected and exciting.

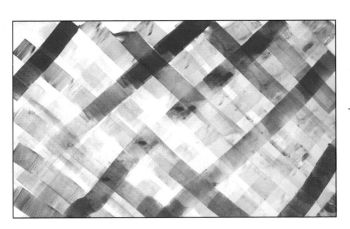

◀ Don't waste paint when it's time to clean your roller! Roll strips onto a large sheet of paper until the color is faint. Now wipe the roller clean and use it for another color. Do the same again, and you'll have a checkerboard pattern — perfect for wrapping paper.

# Multicolored monoprints

MONOPRINTS CAN PRODUCE SUCH wild, unexpected patterns that you can use them as an exciting starting point, and then draw or print your picture into them. Or make a really wonderful print by building up each color separately, with a drawing under the glass slab as a guide.

### PICTURES FROM A MESS!

Perhaps you have printed a real kaleidoscope of mixed-up colors from your slab. Look at it very carefully and you may start to see shapes in it. Try to turn the splodges into plants by adding a few stems and leaves, or make an extraordinary animal by adding some eyes and feet! Maybe it could become an imaginary landscape – an ideal background for a scene of wild beasts or spaceships.

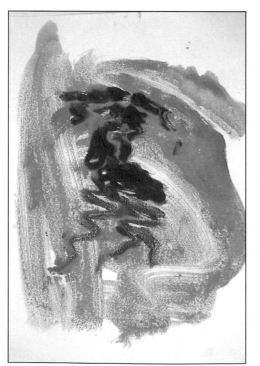

*◄ A wild mixture of paints on the slab makes a colorful, abstract print.*

*► With the first print still wet, a second print can be taken off it by pressing paper onto its surface. With the patterns now simplified, the second print will begin to look like something – here, a few lines drawn with a felt-tip pen makes a Spanish dancer!*

## A THREE-COLOR PRINT

You can make a more complicated monoprint by building up the color in stages. For this you will need a transparent rolling surface (glass or clear plastic are ideal) so that you can place your sketch underneath as a guide. Tape your paper down on one side to make a hinge, so that it goes back in exactly the same position for each inking.

*1 Draw a simple picture on a sheet of paper to act as a guide, and slide it under your glass slab. Put the first color on the slab, in the place where you want it in the picture. Press the paper down carefully and evenly all over. Lift it off and let it dry. Wipe the printing slab clean, and paint in your second color. Take a second print and let it dry again.*

Tape your paper down on one side to keep it in position.

Don't worry about the smudges – they're part of the fun!

*2 Take a third print in the same way. This print is made with three colors — first yellow, then red, then blue — but when you've practiced you can build up even more. Some of your inks will probably print over each other at the edges. This is called "overprinting" and it isn't necessarily a mistake — many printers do it on purpose to make even more colors out of the mixtures.*

▲ *If the ink on your monoprint is really thick, you can lay a sheet of paper on top and make a paler print of your print! It will be reversed.*

143

# Lino cuts

FOR ABOUT A HUNDRED YEARS linoleum has been used to make prints. It was a new material – made from cork and oil – that was used for flooring. It is ideal for detailed cutting and will allow prints to be taken from it again and again, so it has been used by printers ever since. It is a wonderful material to work with – and it even smells pleasant!

## CUTTING A PATTERN

You can buy lino, or use a thick vinyl floor tile. A sharp craft knife will do for simple shapes, but you may want to buy special tools (you can get them at most art shops). It is a good idea to warm the lino before starting – it makes cutting easier.

## CUTTING TIPS

• Special lino tools are very sharp, so practice first to get the feel of them, and find out what marks each tool makes. Always keep both hands behind the blade so that you don't risk cutting yourself.

• Place your block with the top edge against something firm, such as a wall, so it won't slip. This makes cutting much easier.

• Cut away enough background, but make the cuts shallow. Deep cutting will break the string backing of the lino.

• Remember that what you cut away will not print, and will therefore be white in your picture.

## CUTTING THE BLOCK

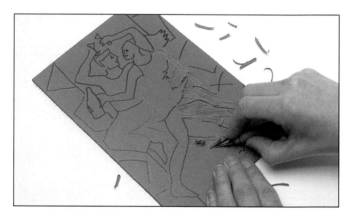

1 *Draw your design on a piece of lino. Cut away the areas and lines you don't want to print.*

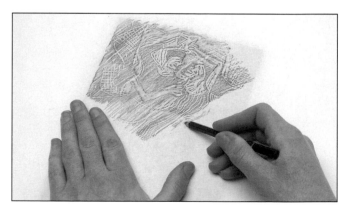

2 *To check what your print will look like, lay a sheet of thin paper over the block and rub all over with a soft pencil. You can still make changes!*

Try printing the same lino cut on different kinds of
paper – colored paper, tracing paper, brown wrapping
paper, or tissue paper – and see the differences. The
thinner the paper, the more detail you'll get – but don't
go too thin, or it might tear.

*3 Spread ink on your inking slab and roll your roller over it to
get a good coating of ink. Roll it evenly over the lino block.*

*4 Lay your paper on top of the inked surface. Smooth it
down with your fingers so there are no air bubbles
underneath. Roll all over it with a clean roller.*

*5 Peel the paper off carefully, starting with one corner, then leave
it to dry. When it is quite dry, you can display it or frame it.*

# Colored lino cuts

NOW YOU HAVE GOT THE BASIC idea of lino cutting (and, with luck, not too many plasters on your fingers!), why not try some more complicated prints. Here are two ways of making multicolored prints from one block.

## CUTTING AWAY TO COLOR

This exciting way of making a colored lino print is called a "reduction" print, because after printing each stage you cut more lino away. Sometimes there is very little left on the block by the end! The Spanish artist Picasso loved using this method – and made some wonderfully bold and vigorous prints.

## GETTING IT IN REGISTER

When you're making several prints to build up lots of colors, you must keep the paper in exactly the same place on the block every time. An easy way to do this is to draw a fine pencil line on your paper round the block. At each stage replace the block exactly inside this outline – but don't do it upside down!

1 First, plan your drawing – this clown print is in red, blue, and turquoise. Cut away the areas you want to leave white, then roll the block evenly with red ink. Take a print and let it dry. Clean the block, then cut away the areas you want to keep red.

2 Roll turquoise ink onto the block and take another print. Remember to place your printing paper in exactly the same place every time. Clean the block again, and this time cut away the areas you want to keep turquoise. Roll the block finally with blue ink, and take the final print.

## A JIGSAW PRINT

Here is another way to make a colored print. With a craft knife, cut a lino block right through into a number of shapes, rather like a simple jigsaw puzzle. Roll different-colored ink onto each piece, and reassemble the puzzle, fitting the pieces closely together. Then take a print.

Roll each piece in a different color.

The white lines where the pieces were fitted back together show up the pattern.

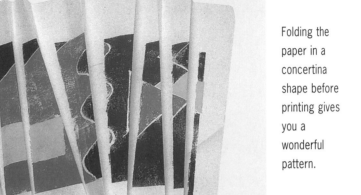

Folding the paper in a concertina shape before printing gives you a wonderful pattern.

3 *Lift off the finished print carefully. The final printing of blue ink has gone on top of the other two colors, so they only show through in certain places. The patterns of color are wonderful.*

# Lino cut experiments

IF YOU HAVE A LINO BLOCK WITH AN image you really like, you can print it in lots of different ways. A lino block is strong enough to be printed again and again. Try printing different colors on top of each other, printing on folded paper, or onto a tissue paper collage. If you have made a monoprint with swirly colors (look at page 59), print your lino cut on top of this and you will have a masterpiece!

Sharp lino prints look great on top of swirly monoprints.

A collage of colored tissue paper makes a brilliant background.

Print some horses fainter so they look far away.

Overlapping some horses makes them look very realistic.

148

## Little "Stained Glass" Windows

The strong printing you get from a black lino cut is a good contrast to colors. Here, a lino-cut print on thick tracing paper gives you the bars in the glass — fill in the spaces with your brightest felt-tip pens. Hang the medallions in front of a window so the light shines through them.

## Making Bags for Presents

Collect paper bags in different sizes and colors, print them with your horse lino cuts, and tie them with matching ribbons. You can add cards and wrapping paper to your "designer" collection.

Cut a rubber horseshoe stamp to print hoofprints.

## Same Blocks — Different Colors

Two blocks — each of a galloping horse — are printed over and over again in different colors on a big sheet of paper. A stampede like this would make a dramatic frieze for your room!

# Signed and sealed

SEALS WERE AMONG THE EARLIEST FORMS of printing and have been used for many thousands of years. A pattern is pressed into warm wax — when the wax cools and hardens, the image is perfectly preserved. Seals can be simple or very ornate; they can be carved onto the ends of wooden knobs, or form part of beautiful jewelry — "signet" rings are those with seals on, for signing letters. Taking shapes in wax or plaster is used for many things — from impressions for false teeth to masks for the theater!

## SEALS OF OLD

Both paper and printing were invented in Northern China, many centuries ago. Chinese nobles had small wooden blocks specially carved with their name or mark, which were dipped in paints made from soot or earth, and stamped onto paper or fabric. Because such seals are hard to forge, they are an important way of showing that something is real and not a copy. Rulers used them to issue laws, and artists to authenticate their work.

## SIMPLE SEALS

Shells, coins, buttons, nuts, bolts, and paper clips all make good impressions in wax.

Corks

Things to stick on the corks

This letter has been sealed with little scraps of dried flowers and leaves, pressed into melted wax.

Sealing wax

The seal used here was made by arranging three little hooks in a pattern.

## SEALED LETTERS

Before the days of gummed envelopes, letters were folded and sealed. If the seal was broken, you knew someone had looked inside! You can either make a seal from sealing wax or use a colored candle.

---

### WHAT YOU NEED

Sealing wax or colored candle wax

Things to press into the wax

Corks to make mounts

Glue

Envelopes, paper, ribbon, string, etc.

---

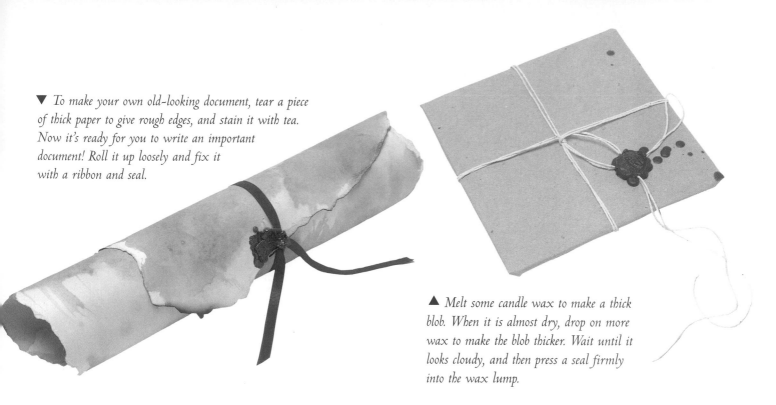

▼ To make your own old-looking document, tear a piece of thick paper to give rough edges, and stain it with tea. Now it's ready for you to write an important document! Roll it up loosely and fix it with a ribbon and seal.

▲ Melt some candle wax to make a thick blob. When it is almost dry, drop on more wax to make the blob thicker. Wait until it looks cloudy, and then press a seal firmly into the wax lump.

## PLASTER OF PARIS IMPRESSIONS

Sometimes a kind of light plaster , known as plaster of Paris, is used to make shapes. For this theater mask, quick-drying rubber was smoothed over the actor's face. When it is peeled off, plaster is poured into the shape. This sets to make an exact copy of the face, and is used to build a mask which will fit perfectly.

Plaster mold from which the mask will be made in a perfect fit.

◄ This half-mask was made for a fairy in "A Midsummer Night's Dream", a play by William Shakespeare. A papier mache shell was molded round the plaster mask, then painted in delicate colors.

# Lasting impressions

LAYING DAMP PAPER OVER different bumps and shapes leaves a permanent impression when the paper dries. This technique can make interesting three-dimensional backgrounds for your pictures, because you can indicate shapes without using any color or lines.

## BRAILLE WRITING

Braille is a system of reading for the blind invented nearly two hundred years ago. Patterns of raised dots represent letters, and people read books by running their fingers over the bumps. It was used by the French general Napoleon to pass silent messages among his soldiers so the enemy wouldn't hear them.

▲ *Braille letters take up a lot of space, so books are enormous. You could invent a simple form of braille and use it as a special code among your friends.*

## PAPER IMPRESSIONS

The patterns in your paper will come out better if you press the shapes into the paper under a really heavy weight. A printing press is ideal.

◀ *Arrange torn paper and card so that there are several levels, but the surface is fairly flat. Dampen a sheet of heavy paper, lay it on top, weight it, and leave it overnight to dry. You will have a different pattern on each side. Complete a picture by painting, or adding colored stencils or stamps.*

## DOUBLE YOUR MONEY!

Make a fairly flat pile of coins. Cover them with a piece of foil, and gently press it onto the pile. Rub the surfaces gently with your fingers through the foil, taking care not to tear it. Soon you'll have an extra pile of silver money!

The patterns on the coins appear on the foil.

## A TREASURE CHEST FOR YOUR MONEY

If you possess a sturdy box, you can easily turn it into a very special money-box. First cut a neat slit in the top. Spread a thin layer of glue all over the box, and press on lots of small coins and money symbols cut out of thick card. Then cut a large sheet of silver foil and wrap the box completely, pressing it in to show up the shapes. If you rub in some dark ink, it will make the foil look old, and adding gold touches will make it look like it is made of precious metal.

### WHAT YOU NEED

Small cardboard box
Sheet of foil
Coins
Cardboard cut-outs
Scissors and glue
Ink and gold felt-tip pen

Money symbols cut from thick card.

153

# Rubbings

MAKING RUBBINGS CAN REALLY FEEL like magic. When you lay a piece of blank paper over a textured object, and rub over it with a crayon or soft pencil, you see a pattern literally appearing before your eyes. Some wonderful rubbings can be made from gravestones in churchyards, but you can make exciting pictures from the simplest things, such as stones or leaves.

▲ *Try making a rubbing from stone, as here, or brick or tree bark with a soft wax crayon in a range of bright colors.*

## WHAT YOU NEED

Wax crayons, candle wax, oil pastel, or anything that is waterproof

Thin paper, white or colored

Paint and brushes

## CHURCHYARD RUBBINGS

Many churchyards contain decorated memorials, sometimes very old and beautiful. To make a really good rubbing, it is worth buying the right materials from an art shop. These include a special sort of wax, which is perfect for bringing out all the details. It is not expensive, and you can get it in many different colors.

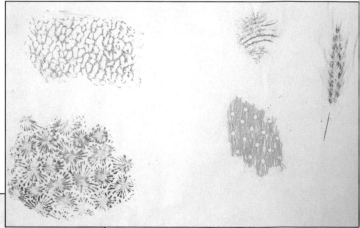

Old window glass sometimes makes good patterns. Tape a sheet of thin paper over the patterned side, and rub with a dark-colored wax crayon.

▲ *Collage blocks — like the string block made on page 35 — make interesting surfaces to rub. Cover the block with a sheet of thin paper, rub it gently with candle wax, and then stain it with thin paint.*

Delicate rubbings from feathers.

Leaves make very good rubbings.

▲ *Collect leaves from a garden or park, and make rubbings with different-colored crayons, or candle wax and stains made with thin paint.*

# Etching and scratching

SOME METHODS OF PRINTING ARE QUITE DANGEROUS. Etchings are made when strong chemicals eat away lines and patterns in metal – the strong fumes mean that etchers usually wear masks and use ventilators. It is something to try if you ever go to art college, but meanwhile you can try something similar by scratching marks onto Perspex and printing them like an etching. This is called drypoint.

Smooth-ended tool for rubbing

Fine scratching tool

### WHAT YOU NEED

Sheet of Perspex or thick plastic

Tools with sharp points, such as a compass or 6in nail

Ink and roller

Old rags

Soft paper for printing

Newspaper

Roller

Colored wax

▲ *The famous seventeenth-century Dutch painter Rembrandt was a superb etcher. Look at how the finest lines came out beautifully in his etching of the Holy Family on the flight into Egypt.*

## SCRATCHING INTO PERSPEX

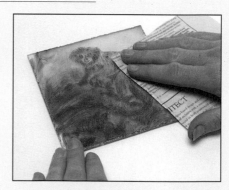

1 *Plan your drawing first, then cover the sheet of plastic with a thin layer of wax. This will enable you to see the marks you scratch. Try to make the marks varied – crisscrossing, deeper or thicker cuts, dots, lines, and dashes. Wipe off the wax and rub ink all over it with a soft rag, pressing it well into the grooves.*

2 *Wipe all the ink off the surface with a piece of folded newspaper held flat. This removes ink only from the surface, because you want to leave all the ink in the grooves.*

## ETCHING WITH A PRESS

◀ *Here is the etching taken from the metal plate. This way of printing allows you to make lines as fine as a hair, or a large block of thick ink. It's a good method for cartoon pictures such as this one.*

This metal plate has been etched with strong chemicals to leave deep grooves. Ink is pressed into these grooves, and smoothed off the shiny surface. A sheet of damp paper is placed on the plate, and the two are put through a heavy press where the ink is squeezed onto the paper.

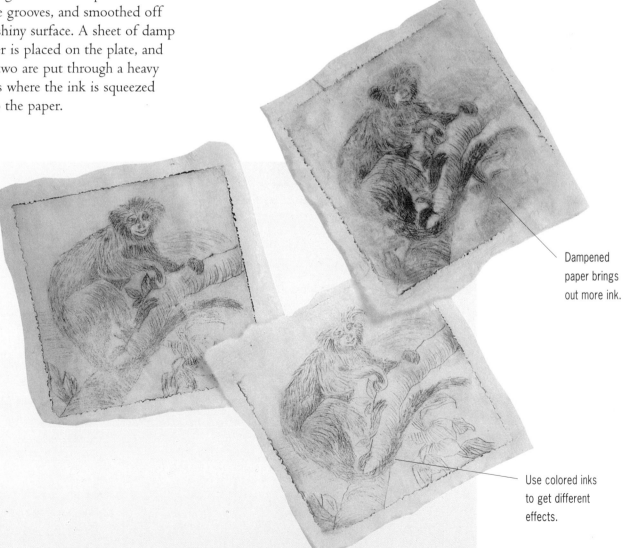

Dampened paper brings out more ink.

Use colored inks to get different effects.

# Silk-screen printing

SILK-SCREEN PRINTING IS A METHOD in which ink is squeezed through a fine mesh screen onto a surface, leaving areas that are masked off unprinted. The result is a pattern of inked and blank shapes. The screen is very fine, so the ink goes onto the paper in a very solid, strong block, with the edges of the pattern clear and crisp.

◀ *Medieval knights wore colored crosses on their tunics. These were early silk-screens, printed by blocking out a cross on a fine fabric screen with pitch or tar, then pressing paint through the mesh.*

## MAKING YOUR OWN SCREEN

If you do not want to buy a silk-screen from an art shop, you can build your own, or get someone to do it for you. You can adapt an old picture frame, but the best frame for stretching the mesh is a rectangle made of 1in (2.5cm) wood. Old net curtain makes a very good mesh screen – make sure it is completely plain.

*1 Make the frame whatever size you want. Wet the net and wring it out so it is evenly damp. Stretch it over the frame as tightly as possible, and secure it all round with a staple gun.*

### WHAT YOU NEED

Wooden frame

Nylon net or muslin

Staple gun

Gum strip

Waterproof PVA medium or varnish

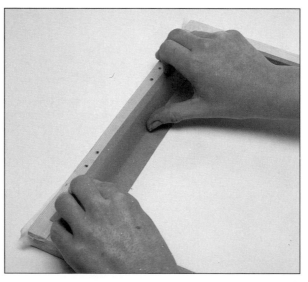

*2 Turn the frame over so the mesh is underneath. Stick gum strip all round the inside edge, so the mesh is joined to the frame. Turn it back over, and stick more gum strip all round to match the first strip. When the strips are dry, paint on PVA medium or varnish to make them waterproof. The whole screen will tighten when it is dry.*

## A TORN PAPER PRINT

Squeegee should be
slightly narrower than
screen.

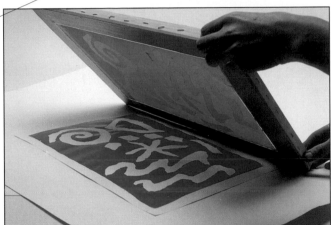

*I* *Put a large sheet of*
*printing paper on a hard,*
*flat base. Arrange torn strips*
*of paper in a pattern on top.*
*Place the screen squarely over*
*this stencil. Pour ink onto the*
*top end of the screen and pull*
*evenly with a squeegee down*
*the surface of the screen,*
*pressing the ink well in. This is*
*easier if you get someone else to*
*hold the screen while you ink.*

*2* *The squeegee forces the ink*
*through the screen onto the*
*paper. It also makes the stencil*
*stick to the screen, so that you*
*can make several prints with*
*the same pattern.*

### SCREEN-PRINTING INKS

Most craft shops sell a special
screen-printing medium. You mix
it with gouache or acrylic
paints to make a thick
waterproof ink, which is an
ideal texture for screen-
printing.

▶*If you put*
*blue ink on the*
*left side of the screen,*
*and yellow on the right, they*
*will mix at the edges when pulled*
*across the mesh, making a stripe of green in*
*the middle.*

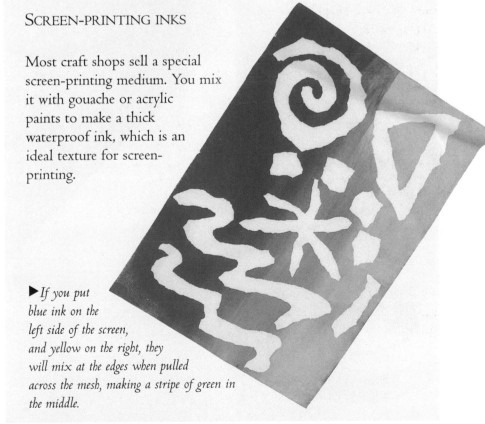

# Multicolored screen-printing

**A** PRINTING SCREEN CAN BE USED over and over again. Water-based inks can be rinsed off under a tap, and then you can start again with another color or design. For complicated color prints, you will need help with holding the screen steady. If you can, get someone who is good at woodwork to make you a hinge to hold the screen up which makes printing easier.

### WHAT YOU NEED
..................................................
Water-based screen-
printing inks
Printing paper
Thin paper for stencil
Craft knife or scissors
Pencil
Sticky tape

A piece of hardboard attached to the bottom of the screen will enable you to make guidelines and keep your print in register.

## PRINTING A TWO-COLOR STENCIL

You can easily build up colored stencils in stages. Draw a simple design and decide at the beginning where you want each color – this is important! Trace the picture and cut out the area to be printed. All the green areas on this stencil have been cut out first. Take the first print – it's a good idea to mark the position of the corners on the frame with sticky tape, so that you get the paper back in exactly the same place for each color.

Attach two pegs with hinges, so that you can prop your screen up.

Sticky tape to mark the corners will keep the print in register.

**I** *When you've printed the first color, trace the areas for the second color (here it is orange) from the design onto a sheet of tracing paper and cut out these spaces. Replace the print on the bed, and place the second stencil on top so the spaces are where you want the orange ink to go.*

Flat, thick color and clean edges are typical of screen-prints.

## USING THE REMAINS

You will have some strange shapes left over after cutting the stencils. Try sticking them on a clean screen, and making another print. You may have some surprises!

*2 Lay the screen on top and pull some orange ink across the mesh with the squeegee. Lift off the print and leave it to dry. When you get good at this, you can add as many colors as you like.*

# Fabric printing

PRINTING YOUR OWN DESIGN IS very exciting if you can then wear it! Most of the printing you have tried so far has been on paper, but you can also make prints on fabric, foil, or even plastic. Repeat your print along a length of fabric, and you have made your own dressmaking material. You can also print T-shirts with individual patterns.

## WHAT YOU CAN PRINT ON

Fabric for printing needs to be fairly fine weave — this makes the design clearer. New fabric should be washed first to soften it and allow it shrink. Old net curtains and gauze make excellent printing materials.

As you repeat the printing, the colors will fade.

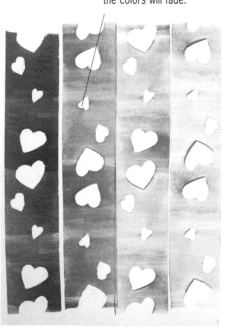

## PRINTING FABRIC

Cut heart shapes out of a large sheet of tracing paper or newspaper to make a stencil. Lay the fabric smoothly on the base of the frame, cover with the stencil, close the screen, and pour printing ink across the top of the screen. Pull this firmly down the mesh with a squeegee. Keep moving the fabric along in the frame to repeat the pattern down its length.

Heart stencil for printing

▲ *Printing a T-shirt is very easy and looks marvelous. This one has been printed with the torn paper stencil shown on page 75. Put a sheet of card inside the T-shirt so that the fabric stays taut and print in exactly the same way as on paper.*

## DRAWING ON YOUR SCREEN

You can draw directly onto the mesh screen with water-based crayons (they'll wash off afterwards). Then, instead of ink or paint, you press wallpaper paste through the screen with the squeegee. The paste dissolves the crayon colors through the screen onto the paper beneath. This is almost like doing a painting, but the screen mesh gives the areas of paint a texture like fabric. You can get beautiful effects with sweeps of mixed color, and areas of fine detail.

1 *First draw your picture directly onto the mesh screen.*

2 *Use lots of different bright colors to get the best effect.*

3 *Mix wallpaper paste till it's creamy, and press it through the mesh.*

4 *Lift up the screen and remove the picture carefully.*

# Fancy dress

PRINTING ALLOWS YOU TO MAKE wonderful things very quickly and often cheaply. You can cover large areas of paper or fabric at great speed, and create exotic costumes for yourself and your friends, so it's great for dressing up. If you use old materials, you do not have to worry that they will not last – just make more!

## QUEEN OF HEARTS

"The Queen of Hearts, she made some tarts . . ." You can print all you need for this costume, and finish it with a decorated crown.

Crown made from cardboard, covered in foil, and decorated with hearts.

Jam tarts printed with potato blocks.

▲ *Make a pinafore with printed heart material — an old sheet would be ideal.*

# PIRATE

A pirate costume is easy to put together — old trousers and a shirt, wellington boots and a colored scarf. But how about making a brilliant parrot to sit on your shoulder, a skull-and-crossbones flag, and an old map showing how to find the hidden treasure?

▲ *Look at page 28 for how to print feathers. Draw the outline of a parrot on a piece of card and fill it with brightly colored feather prints. Add details with felt-tip pens and attach wire to the back with tape, so it can sit on your shoulder.*

▲ *Draw a map of hidden treasure on a sheet of torn paper stained with tea to look old, and close it with a seal. Page 67 shows you how to do this.*

# Lithography

ONE METHOD OF PRINTING USED by some famous artists is lithography, which means "drawing on stone." It is said to have been invented hundreds of years ago by a playwright who scribbled his laundry list on a stone, then found the image had printed in reverse onto some clothes. The modern version of this is called photolithography — inked images are put onto a huge roller and then transferred to the paper. This means that the image can be printed the right way round.

▲ *Modern four-color printing machines — such as the one shown here — give very fine adjustments to how strong the inks will be. Someone must still check the prints, however!*

## LITHOGRAPHY — HOW SEPARATE COLORS ARE PUT TOGETHER

A lithograph is made by drawing or painting with greasy ink on a metal plate. This then goes through lots of processes, so that the printing ink will stick to the drawn areas and wash off all the rest. A heavy roller passes over the inked plate, and transfers the inky picture onto a sheet of paper. There has to be a separate plate for each color — it could be as many as 12. All the different colors — together with any new colors made by blendings — build up to make the finished picture.

The main background color is printed first.

The red plate is printed next.

The green plate is printed last.

▼ *Repeats of the same pattern can look great when built up with different colors.*

◄ *This lithograph of cows in a field was made from separate color plates. Where they have overlapped and printed on top of each other, they make even more colors. Lithographs often have a very attractive soft texture.*

► *The French painter Toulouse-Lautrec loved lithography. How many different colors can you count in his image called "The Jockey"?*

◄ *This lithograph of peppers and tomatoes was made from three color plates. Look how the three colors mix together to make different shades of brown for the shadows. This mixing to make new colors is one of the exciting things about multicolored printing - you never quite know what's going to happen!*

## PRINTING WITH A PRESS

Most serious printers use a press to make their prints. This puts an enormous amount of pressure onto the printing block, so that even the most delicate marks, textures, and patterns are squeezed onto the paper.

Experiment with your prints by using different amounts of pressure, then compare the results.

# Wood works

ALL PRINTING USED TO BE DONE with wood – some of the most beautiful illustrations in old books were made from wooden blocks carved in the most intricate detail. In some countries they still use wood blocks for printing on fabric. You can cut very fine lines on wood, and make its grainy texture part of the pattern.

▲ *Thomas Bewick was a remarkable wood engraver who lived 300 years ago in England. He illustrated many books with pictures of animals and birds. He used a very hard wood called boxwood for his prints – one of his printing blocks was used 900,000 times!*

## WHAT YOU NEED

Piece of balsa wood

Tools, such as a knife, knitting needle, etc.

Inked slab

Rollers

Paper

## MAKING A WOOD BLOCK

Because it lasts so well, a wood block is a good choice for a design you want to keep and use over and over again. So it's worth taking care to get it right – make practice sketches before you finalize your design.

▲ *When you're happy with your design, cut round the edges with a sharp knife. You could also press lines in the wood with a knitting needle.*

Remember that the finished image will print in reverse.

The block needs plenty of ink, as wood is absorbent.

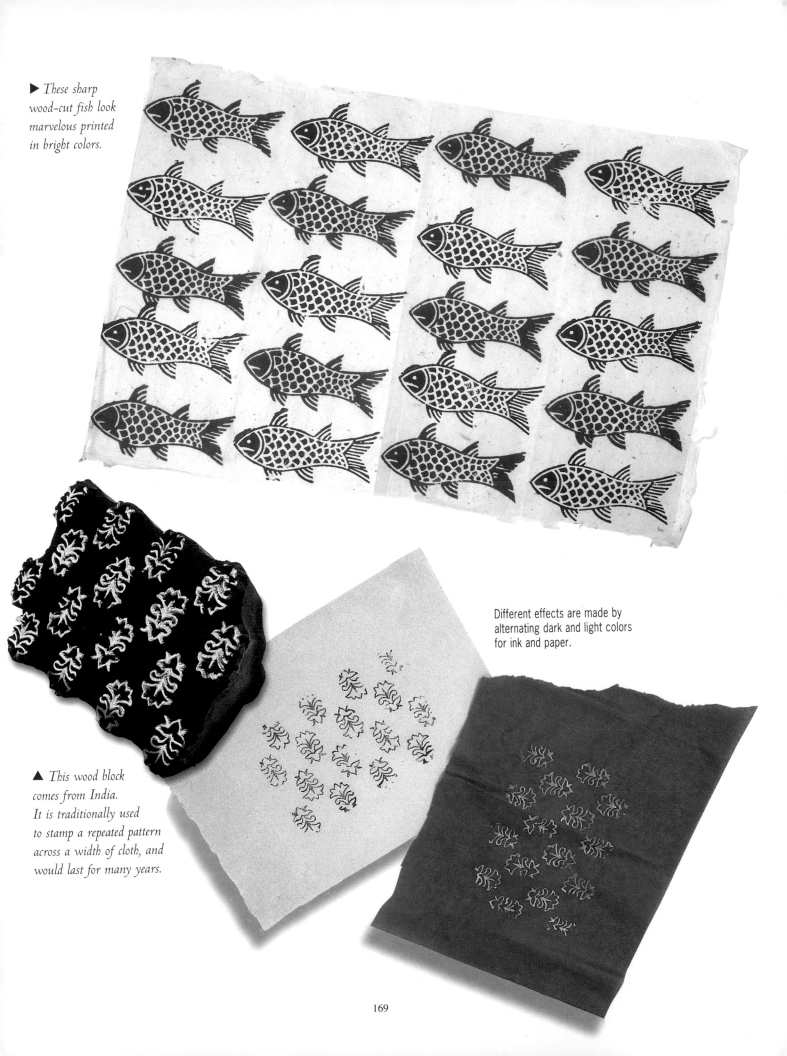

▶ *These sharp wood-cut fish look marvelous printed in bright colors.*

Different effects are made by alternating dark and light colors for ink and paper.

▲ *This wood block comes from India. It is traditionally used to stamp a repeated pattern across a width of cloth, and would last for many years.*

# Living in print

Now you have tried lots of ways of printing, you could combine different methods to decorate your room in a very special way. It will not cost a lot, so you can easily change it when you want to try out new ideas.

## DECORATE YOUR ROOM

Bedroom, classroom, den — anywhere that needs a bit of living up can be transformed by your printing efforts. Here are just a few ideas: stenciled or printed floors or furniture; printed bedclothes, cushions, or curtains; folders and books covered with marbled paper; leaf prints on walls; prints on mirrors and windows.

▲ *See how good the lino-cut horse (from page 64) looks when it is printed on wood. The grain showing through adds to its effect. If you find a piece of unpainted wood no one wants, print a group of horses galloping along it.*

## STARS AT NIGHT

Invisible in the light, luminous paint comes to life after dark. If you can get permission, try decorating the ceiling of your room with moons and stars glowing in a deep blue sky!

### WHAT YOU NEED

Luminous paint
Paint brush
Printing blocks
A firm ladder
Someone to help you!

*Make card printing blocks of planets, stars, moons, and rockets. Plan your design carefully, then print the blocks on the ceiling using luminous paint. Wait until dark!*

## SPECIAL BOXES

Do not throw away prints you dislike or consider failures — they can often be useful. You can make a colorful set of storage boxes in different sizes, by using shoe boxes, chocolate boxes, and anything else you can find. Transform them with a patchwork of printed paper. Seal them with varnish or diluted PVA medium and they will last a long time.

▲ *Here is a special box for your diary or other secret things. It is covered with foil imprinted with the shape of a question mark. You could mark your other boxes with secret signs that only you will understand.*

▶ *You can make lovely frames for your best prints — and your favorite photos and treasures — from cardboard stuck with shapes and covered with inked foil.*

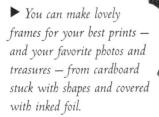

### MORE IDEAS

• Keep one print from all your blocks, stamps, and other techniques in a special book or folder. Even when they have worn out or been thrown away, you'll still have a record of every one.
• Use stencils to make a pattern on a plain lampshade, or stencil narrow strips of paper to make a frieze round a window or door.
• Print your name on your door using your set of stenciled letters.

# Print celebrations

Festivals and celebrations are a great opportunity to use your printing skills. Printing allows you to make things in quantity, like sets of Christmas cards or party invitations. And once you have a shape or an image you really like, you can make prints on lots of things. A themed party is easy this way!

Gold holly stencils make red balloons look Christmassy!

## PARTIES

Print invitations, paper plates, and mugs (waterproof paint only!). Decorate balloons with glitter paint shapes — blow up a balloon, print a shape on it using glue, and sprinkle glitter over it. Print a line of rubber stamp prints as a decoration for thank-you letters, and close them with a personal seal.

## FEASTS AND HOLIDAYS

Christmas and other big feasts are a chance to go wild and fill the house with printed decorations. You can make paper chains — print sheets of colored paper with gold stars, cut them into equal strips, and make them into a chain. For Easter, paint some blown eggs and decorate them with tiny rubber stamp designs.

Holly stencils can be made into a paper chain.

# PRINTED PRESENTS WRAPPED IN PRINT

People always love receiving handmade presents – and you can wrap them in hand-patterned paper and add your own handmade cards, too.

◀ *This picture frame is made with printed feathers and rubber stamp diamonds. The image inside is a silk-screen Christmas tree which you can put on matching wrapping paper.*

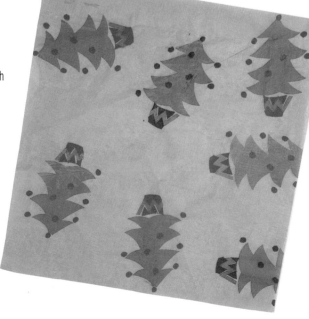

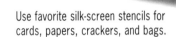

Use favorite silk-screen stencils for cards, papers, crackers, and bags.

A range of papers with matching prints in different colors.

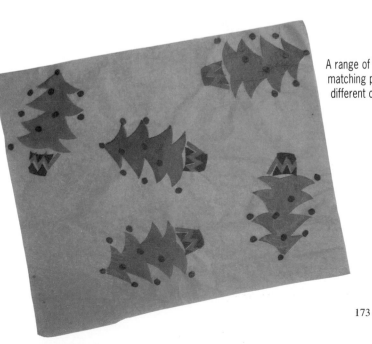

# Finishing work

THE VERY BEST PRINTERS ARE THOSE WHO clean up after work, put tops on paints, wash brushes, clean surfaces and tools, and store work safely. Can you imagine what the very worst are like? If you store your prints carefully you will have a collection of wonderful things to use now and lots of fun later!

## MAKING A SCRAP BOOK OR FOLDER

Use stiff cardboard to make the folder and cover it with paper. Stick a favorite print on the front, or decorate the whole cover with a pattern of rubber stamps. Attach some tape or ribbon to close the folder, and fill it with your best work.

---

### WHAT YOU NEED
..................................................
Large sheet of paper

Two sheets of cardboard the same size

Tape or ribbon

Glue

---

▲ *Keep your best prints to mount on colored card, either to display, or to send to friends.*

## DRYING PRINTS

In printers' studios you will often see a row of prints hanging up to dry in a special rack. But you can easily dry prints by hanging them to some string with clothes pegs. You might find a print is bumpy and crinkled. Don't worry – lay it under a flat board with some heavy weights on top for a couple of hours.

## USING PRINTS
## YOU DON'T LIKE

Don't throw away any failures. Cut them up into small shapes and glue them onto a big sheet of paper to make "patchwork" paper. You can use this to cover boxes, make a screen, or wrap presents.

## FAMOUS PRINTERS

Now you know a little bit about printing, you may enjoy seeing prints in museums and galleries, and come away with lots of good ideas. Many museums have special print rooms but you might have to get special permission to visit them. Some museums have special exhibitions of printing.

Famous artists who were specially interested in printmaking include Albrecht Dürer in the fifteenth century, Rembrandt in the seventeenth century, Toulouse-Lautrec in the nineteenth century, and Henri Matisse, Edvard Munch, Pablo Picasso, and Andy Warhol in the twentieth century. Have a look at their work in books – it may give you some ideas.

# PAPERCRAFT

## MOIRA BUTTERFIELD

# CONTENTS

## Papercraft

# All about paper

PAPER IS MADE FROM WOOD, PLANT, or rag fibers, and was invented in China over 2,000 years ago. The ideas in this book will introduce you to a world of new paper art possibilities. It's a good idea to learn about basic techniques, but remember you can also have a lot of fun experimenting.

## FINDING THE GRAIN

When paper is made mechanically, its fibers tend to line up in one direction. This is called the "grain." Paper folds, tears, and bends more easily in this direction. For complicated projects involving paper-folding, it is often important to find the grain before you start.

## DIFFERENT PAPER AND CARD

Generally, the stronger paper is, the better it will be at holding a crease or fold, which is important for paper art. There's a wide range of paper and card you can use. Here we show you some of the main types – all of them are easy to buy.

▶ *Crepe paper is stretchy and crinkly. You can buy it in lots of colors.*

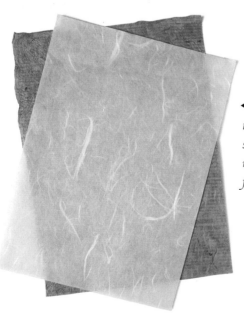

◀ *Japanese paper is thin but very strong, because it is made from long fibers.*

◀ *Medium-weight paper, such as ordinary writing paper, can be painted if it has an absorbent, dull ("matt") surface.*

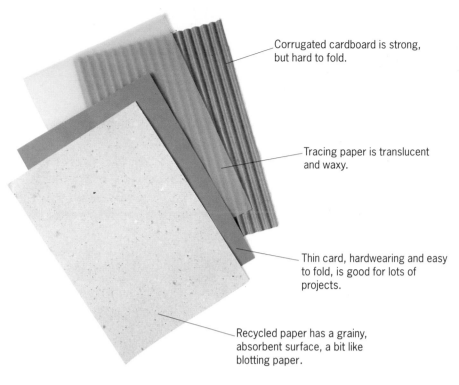

Corrugated cardboard is strong, but hard to fold.

Tracing paper is translucent and waxy.

Thin card, hardwearing and easy to fold, is good for lots of projects.

Recycled paper has a grainy, absorbent surface, a bit like blotting paper.

◀ *Tissue paper is thin, see-through, and delicate. It tears easily.*

◀ *Handmade paper is thick, with many different kinds of decorative surface.*

◀ *Stencil card is a kind of waxy, thin cardboard, that won't absorb water.*

## PAPERCRAFT TOOLS

Here are the main tools needed for the projects in this book. A sturdy metal ruler is better than a plastic one, and safer when you are using a knife. A cutting mat, to protect the surface of your desk or table, can be made of plastic, or you can make your own from several layers of cardboard glued or taped together. Always work on a cutting mat when using a craft knife.

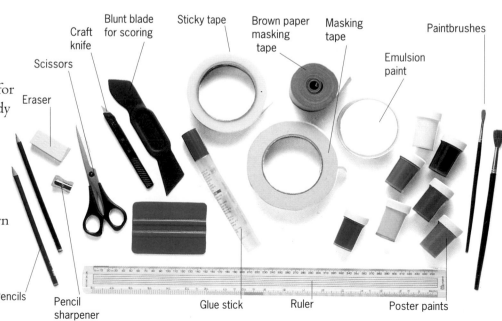

Eraser

Scissors

Craft knife

Blunt blade for scoring

Sticky tape

Brown paper masking tape

Masking tape

Paintbrushes

Emulsion paint

Pencils

Pencil sharpener

Glue stick

Ruler

Poster paints

# Start here

MOST OF THE IDEAS FEATURED in this book use one or more of these basic techniques. Spend a few minutes practicing each one before you go on to more ambitious projects. Whatever you try, always remember the most important rule of papercraft: "Don't rush it!"

## FOLDING

It's a good idea to make folds by laying your paper against a hard surface, such as the top of a table. This helps you to get a neat edge.

▶ *A fold that peaks upwards into an upside-down V-shape is called a "mountain fold."*

▶ *A fold that dips down into a V-shape is called a "valley fold."*

## SCORING

Scoring weakens thick paper or card slightly along a line on one side, so it is easier to make a straight, sharp fold. Always score on the side of the paper that will be on the inside.

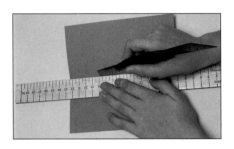

*1 With a ruler as a guide, run the end of a pair of scissors along your fold line.*

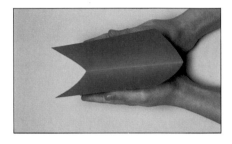

*2 Bend along the scored line. The paper or card will hold the fold neatly in place.*

## PLEATING

Lots of parallel score lines close together enable you to make paper pleats. Practice on square piece of paper, and then on a round piece.

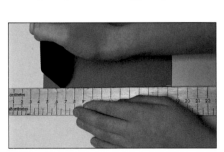

*1 Mark the top and bottom of each fold line, to guide the ruler as you score.*

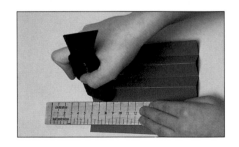

*2 Turn the paper over after each score line, so that you make pleats.*

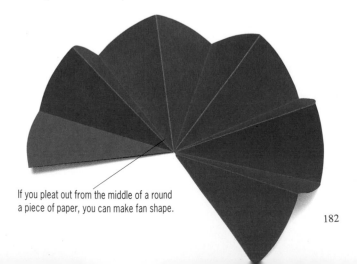

If you pleat out from the middle of a round a piece of paper, you can make fan shape.

Scoring alternately on each side of the paper means you make mountain folds followed by valley folds (see above).

## CURLING

You can use curled paper for all kinds of projects, including paper hair, present decorations, and 3D pictures. Thin paper is easier to curl than thick paper.

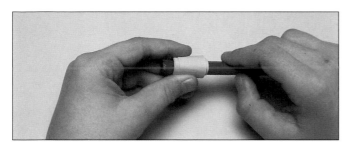

*I* *Wind a long paper strip tightly round a pencil. Keep it wound up tightly for a minute or so, holding it in place with your finger and thumb.*

Use paper curls for hair and eyebrows.

Cut a small cross shape into the paper and open out the flaps for stars.

If you are using scissors, keep cut-out shapes simple.

*2* *Release the paper. If the curl is not tight enough, lay the pencil across the front of the paper, and pull the strip gently toward you under the pencil a few times.*

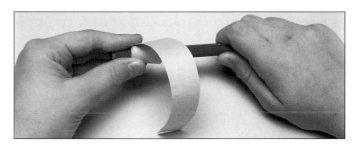

▲ *Depending on how hard you wind the paper, you can make loose curls...*

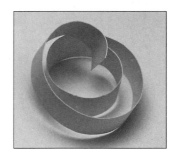

▲ *...or tight curls. This gives a variety of different effects in your pictures.*

## CUTTING

To cut holes out of paper you need small sharp scissors, or a craft knife for more complicated shapes. If you use a craft knife you must use a hard board or a cutting mat (see page 11), to prevent damaging the surface underneath. To cut accurately, pencil guidelines lightly on the paper before you start.

◀ *This night scene is backed with shiny silver paper (you could use foil) to give a glittering effect.*

# Folds and fans

Whent paper is pleated, each mountain fold is followed by a valley fold. In other words, you must fold first to one side of the paper and then the other. You will get the most accurate effect if you measure the folds to keep them even, and score the fold lines (see page 12), but it's not absolutely necessary. Start by practicing pleats on scrap paper, and then try some of the projects shown here.

## PLEAT CUTTING

If you cut into pleated paper, you can make very interesting shapes and patterns. Experiment with different shapes, and then push in or pull out the paper in between the cuts. Think of ways you might use these effects on a greetings card, poster, or painting, perhaps by mounting the pleats on contrasting paper.

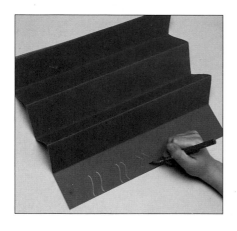

1 *Make marks evenly and lightly across the width of a pleated sheet of paper. These will be a guide for where to make decorative cuts through the pleats.*

2 *Pinch together a pleat and cut into it. Start with some straight cuts, then make cuts of different shapes on each pleat. Try zigzags, curves, and sloping cuts.*

3 *Open the cuts gently, taking care not to tear the paper. Mount your pleated "picture" on a contrasting color of card, so that the pattern shows through.*

## FOLDED FLOWERS

Pleated paper makes good, simple flower shapes.
To display them in a vase, glue the flower
"heads" onto circles of card. Then glue two
circles together back to back, with a plant stick in
between so that they stand up.

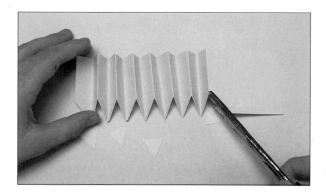

*1 Cut two strips of paper each about 2 x 16 inches. Make
0.5-inch pleats along the narrow edges of both strips of
paper. With sharp scissors, snip a corner off the top of each
pleat. Open up the pleated strips. Curve them round so that
they make circles, and glue them together at both ends.*

*2 When they are dry, mount them on circles of card. Glue
two flower circles together, back to back, with a thin plant
stick in between. Last, screw up little balls of contrasting
tissue paper and glue these to the centers of the flowers.*

▶ *Stand your flowers in a vase to display
them to best effect.*

Pleated paper looks
like flower heads

Use thin. light plant
sticks for the stalks

Tissue paper balls
make the centers

185

# Fans and concertinas

PLEATED PAPER CAN BE USED FOR all kinds of things, from a simple decorative fan to a card! These cards are called "concertinas" because the folds look like the middle part of the musical instrument.

## CONCERTINA CARD

The card here is made with a jungle theme, but you can change that to any subject you like by cutting the pages into different shapes and painting different pictures. Concertina cards make very good celebration cards, and they stand up on their own.

*1 Measure along the card's long edges, making marks every 5 inches on the top and bottom. Score between the first pair of marks. Turn the card over, and score between the next pair of marks.*

*2 Turn over again for the third pair, and over again for the last. Then fold the card up in this order — valley fold, mountain fold, valley fold, mountain fold. This will give a zig-zag effect.*

*3 On the smallest fold, draw a seated animal no taller than 2 inches. Cut round the shape to the folded spine and fold the card up again. Repeat on the next fold but this time make your animal a bit bigger than the last one — they should each look over the last one's shoulder!*

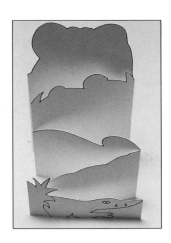

*4 Using your crayons, felt tips, or paints, decorate the paper concertina. Here we have used greens for a jungle scene, and painted it full of colorful animals.*

Add jungle animals to your forest scene

The crocodile makes a good front cover!

# FABULOUS FANS

Pleated paper fans have been made for centuries. Here are some ways you can make your own elegant versions. You can use any paper as long as it holds a pleat well. If you like, paint colorful pictures on your paper before you start.

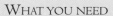

**1** *Pleat a rectangle of colorful paper along the long edge, starting and finishing with a mountain fold. The pleats shown here are 0.75 inches wide.*

**2** *Bunch the pleats together, and fold the strip over at the center. Bring the two long edges together so that they touch, then glue them together from top to bottom.*

A neat hole punched through the end makes it easier to tie tightly with some ribbon.

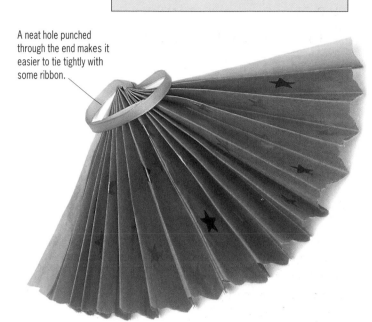

**3** *To make decorative holes, pinch the fan pleats together and snip small triangles evenly out of the front edges. Tie the bottom with ribbon or braid.*

**4** *Open out the fan. Trim back the glued seam so that it does not show through the center hole when the fan is open.*

If you like, thread some pretty braid or ribbon through the holes for a final decoration.

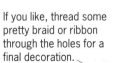

A fan decorated with beautiful ribbon makes a special present.

187

# Quilling

Quilling means winding strips of colored paper into different-shaped coils. You can use them for decoration, and even for making pictures. It takes a little while to do, but it's great fun and very satisfying!

**WHAT YOU NEED**

Strips of colored paper 0.25 inch wide, and as long as you like – bigger strips make bigger coils

Glue and fine-pointed gluebrush

Cocktail stick or thin straw

Backing card to glue your coils on

Make your paper quills into whatever shapes you like.

## QUILLING PICTURES

Quilling pictures are best made with subjects that have curvy shapes that can be easily quilled – circles and ovals, for example. But you can always draw and paint some details and use quilling for others. First, sketch out your picture roughly on medium-weight card and make all the tight and loose coils you need. Glue them to the picture and then finish it off.

▲ *Trees make good subjects for quilling patterns. Birds, sheep with curly fleece, peacock tails, and fish are also ideal.*

*1 Make two slits about 0.25 inch deep in the top of a straw.*

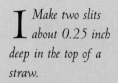

*2 Slot one end of your paper strip into the slits and wind the strip round and round the straw.*

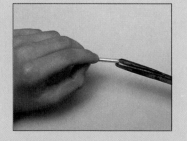

▲ *Make pretty gift tags by sticking coils onto folded card.*

## PHOTO FRAME

You can adapt quilling to decorate
a cardboard frame for your favorite
photograph.

### WHAT YOU NEED

Two pieces of medium-weight colored card, each 6 x 8 inches

Glue and glue brush

Ruler and pencil

Colored paper quilling strips

Sharp scissors, or craft knife and cutting board

*1 On one piece of card measure an area that is the same size as the photograph you want to display in the frame. Make sure to leave an outer margin around it of about 1.5 inches.*

*2 On the second piece of contrasting card, mark out the same area and cut the central part out carefully using a craft knife with a cutting mat underneath to protect your work surface.*

*3 Arrange the quilling on the frame. Brush glue to the back of the coils and fix them in place. Use tweezers to place them exactly where you want them, then press down gently but firmly.*

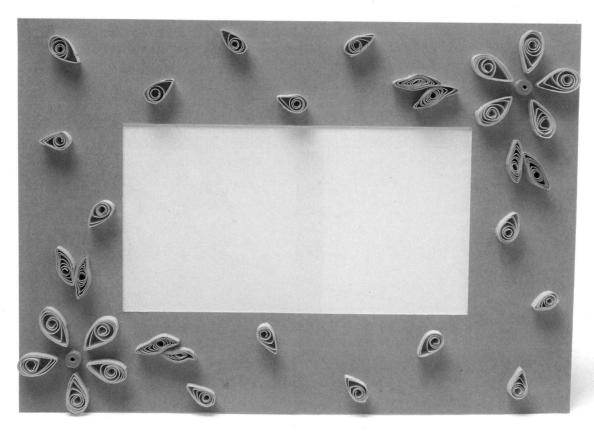

▲ *Run a thin line of glue along three edges of the back of the frame and press it carefully down onto the piece of backing card. When it is dry, slide in your photo through the unglued edge.*

# Perfect planes

USE YOUR PAPER-FOLDING SKILLS to become an airplane inventor. Try the basic designs shown here and then build on them by adding tails, cutting flaps, or folding the paper slightly differently to get varying nose and wing shapes. Flight-test your inventions to see how they perform!

## DART AND STUNT PLANE

As a paper plane travels, air pushes up against the wings. The basic dart is a sharp, streamlined shape, so it slices through the air fast and straight like an arrow. The stunt plane, with wider wings, floats rather than flies, and travels for a longer distance. To get pinpoint accuracy, score the creases first.

## DART

1 Fold the paper in half lengthwise. Unfold it and fold one corner into the middle so that the edge meets the crease.

2 Fold the other corner in to meet the center crease, making sure you keep the point at the top neat and sharp.

3 Keeping the folds you have made in place, fold the same corners down to the middle again.

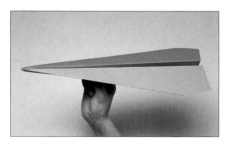

4 Turn the paper over, and fold it up along the original center crease mark. To fly the dart, hold it underneath and launch it upwards.

Experiment with different-shaped rectangles of paper to get different flight paths!

e left corner up to
fthand turn, or
t corner for a
nd turn.

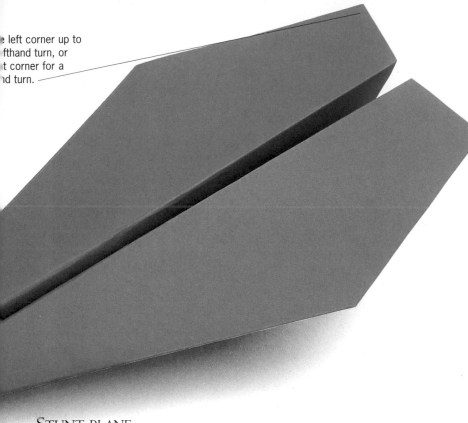

## STUNT PLANE

By adding a tail or flaps, you can alter the way the air
acts on your plane to make it do different stunts.

1 Follow steps 1 and 2 of the dart,
then fold the triangle over. Fold the
two new top corners into the center to
make a flat end at the top.

2 Fold the center point up to make a
tab. You can unfold the top corners
when doing this, as here, but you must
fold them over again and under the tab.

3 Fold the two outer edges into the
central crease, leaving the flat top.
Take time to do this accurately so that
all the folds are sharp and straight.

4 Fold outward along the center crease.
When you turn the stunt plane
over, unfold the wings. It will look like
the finished dart at the top of the page.

## SPINNING HELICOPTER

Drop this helicopter down from
a height and watch it spin fast as
it falls. It's one of the quickest
and easiest toys you can make!

### WHAT YOU NEED

Strip of thin card 1 x 3.5 inches long
Scissors or craft knife
Ruler
Paper clip

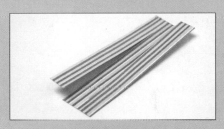

1 Cut two straight 3-inch slits in the
card, one on either side.

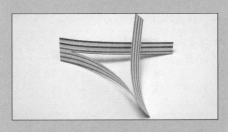

2 Hold the top right corner and the
bottom left corner. Pull them together
to make a triangle shape.

3 Push the paper clip up over the two
ends. Drop the helicopter with the
paper clip pointing
downwards.

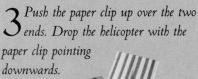

191

# Beautiful boats

W ITH A FLOTILLA OF BRIGHTLY decorated paper boats you and your friends can hold your own racing regatta! Line the boats up on a smooth floor, and flap a magazine up and down behind them to create enough breeze to get them going.

## PAPER BOAT

Experiment with different-sized rectangles to get different-shaped boats, all using the same basic design. Practice using newspaper before you move onto more high-quality paper.

**1** Fold the rectangle in half widthwise. With the fold at the top, turn the two top corners down to the center.

**2** Fold up one bottom edge to make a flap. Turn the boat over and fold up the other edge to make another flap.

**3** Fold the corners back on either side and tape them flat. You need to turn the boat over to do the underside flap.

**4** Hold the taped corners and push them together (halfway through this stage you have a Robin Hood hat!).

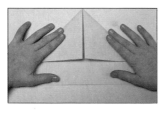

**5** You should then have a square with two triangular flaps. Fold up the flaps on either side to the top.

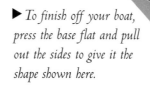

**6** Now you should have a triangle. Push the lower corners together to make the flat square shown above.

▶ To finish off your boat, press the base flat and pull out the sides to give it the shape shown here.

**7** Pull the top points apart sideways. You should then see a triangular "sail" pop out from the base of the boat.

Sail stands up straight from the base of the boat

## RIGGED SAILING SHIP

This ship has sails made from fine, cream-colored paper to look like real canvas. First draw or paint a ship on the background paper, including the masts and the rigging (all the ropes), but leaving off the sails that are fixed to the masts.

### WHAT YOU NEED

Good-quality thick paper for sails
Thick, rubbery-textured glue and glue brush
Pencil, scissors, and ruler
Fine felt-tips or paints
Rectangle of good-quality paper for background
Piece of card to mount the picture

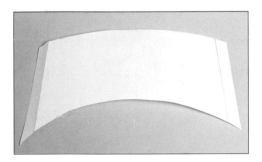

*I First sketch your sail shape, then cut it out with some extra at each side. Fold back the extra width to make tabs. Make big, medium and small sails, and decorate them if you like.*

*2 Fold back the tabs on either side of the sails. Brush these with glue and stick the sails on your picture so they curve outwards. For a finishing touch, mount your picture on contrasting card, smoothing it flat.*

# Paper people

It's easy to make paper people, using paper scraps or card cut from empty food packets. Use them as decorations (in a Christmas crib scene, for example) or as 3D works of art. To give them character, add paper clothes and facial features such as paper noses. When you have practiced a bit with basic shapes, use your imagination to create your own unique people.

## CONE PERSON

Make cone-shaped bodies from paper and stick on contrasting-colored paper pieces for decoration, clothes, and hair. You can also paint on clothes and funny faces.

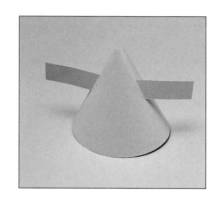

**1** *Cut a semi-circle of paper and curve it round in a cone. Mark arm positions, open out the paper and cut two small arm slits. Curve the cone again and tape the edges together, then slot through a strip for the arms.*

**2** *Make a smaller cone for the head and glue on curled strips of paper for hair (see page 13). Make a skirt by pleating a curved strip of colored paper and glueing it round the cone body. Paint or draw on a face.*

## CYLINDER PERSON

The cylinder person is made in a similar way to the cone person, but with a straight strip of paper that makes a tube shape when curved round. Always check details like armhole positions before you tape the person together at the back.

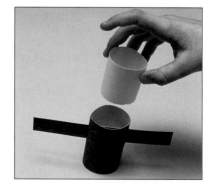

**1** *Cut a paper strip and curve it round into a tube, with an arm strip slotted in as for the cone person above. Make a slightly smaller cylinder for the head and glue it in place.*

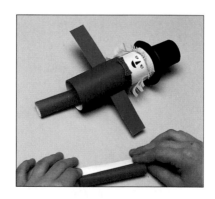

**2** *Curve two strips of paper into tubes for the legs, and glue them to the inside of the body. For a hat, make the head extra long, then push a circle of paper down on it for the brim.*

Why not display your figures in a toy theater? Cut out one of the big sides of a cereal packet — the remaining three sides make a good stage! Glue paper pieces onto the back and sides to make scenery. Then place your figures in position on the base.

▼ *This chapel scene has a "stained glass" window in the background made from pieces of colored tissue paper. It looks very effective when light shines through!*

Hair is made from curled strips of paper.

Buttons are made from circles of paper, slit to the center, and curved round in shallow cone shapes.

Draw your own funny faces!

# Letter Lady

WHAT YOU NEED

Empty cereal packet, or similar card box
Smaller, shallow box
Glue
Ruler
Scissors
Colored paper or paints for
decoration

PAPER PEOPLE CAN BE USEFUL AS WELL AS decorative. Here we show you how to make a letter lady to store your mail, and some unusual pieces of paper jewelry to wear, and give your friends as presents.

## LETTER LADY

This letter holder lady is made from stiff card decorated with paint and brightly colored paper. To make her look realistic, add a paper cone nose and a collar frill. Instead of a stand, you could make a hole in her hat and hang her on the wall or your pinboard. Store letters or pens and pencils in her pocket.

1 *Cut out one big side of a cereal box, together with one of the attached narrow edges to make a stand. Draw a figure on the blank side and cut round it. Decorate the lady with cut-out paper pieces, or paint her. Fold the flap to the back along the crease so that it makes a base enabling her to stand upright.*

2 *Cut out one side of a shallow box, leaving a narrow margin before all the folded edges. Cut off one narrow edge completely. The margin round three sides make tabs that you can glue to the lady's skirt. The narrow edges give you a pocket big enough to put things in.*

3 *For a stand, bend the flap at the bottom of the lady's skirt to the back, so that she stays upright.*

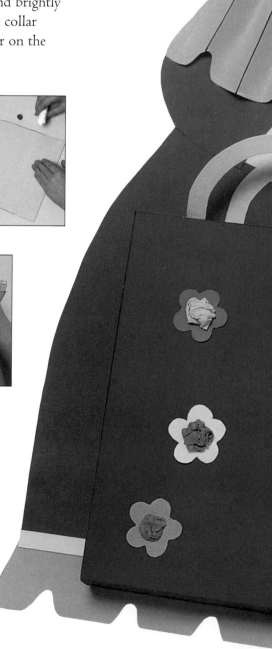

## MINI-PEOPLE

These mini-people, made from card and fabric, are based on traditional jewelry made in South America. Here, they have been used as decoration on a triangular-shaped badge and a matching necklace.

### WHAT YOU NEED

Strips of paper 6 x 1 inches

Scraps of fabric (cut with pinking shears to stop the edges fraying)

PVA glue

Felt-tip pens

Card (cut from an old packing box)

Safety pin or badge bar

Sticky tape

1 *Wrap a strip of thin card into a tight cylinder and tape it in place. Glue a strip of fabric or ribbon round the card cylinder, leaving a short length of card sticking up. Draw a face on this. Make enough mini-people to cover the size you want your badge and necklace to be.*

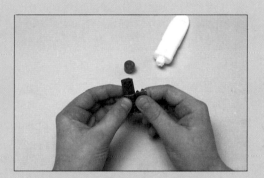

2 *Cut the card into badge and necklace shapes. Paint them and cover them with PVA glue. Stick your mini-people onto them. When the badge is dry, tape or glue a safety pin or badge bar on the back. Punch a hole in each end of the necklace and thread it with cotton to tie round your neck.*

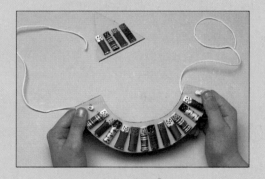

This slot is for storing letters in.

This is a good way to use up scraps of brightly colored ribbon.

197

# Pop-up cards

**M**AKE YOUR OWN CARDS TO GIVE at celebration times. Use your imagination to make designs that are particularly suited to the people who will receive them. They will be extra-special because you've taken time and trouble over them! You can use the ideas in this section to make unusual art pictures, too.

## POP-UPS

There are two basic techniques for making pop-up pictures. Practice them both on scrap paper before you design your own card. Wherever the instructions tell you to fold a line, remember to score it first (see the instructions on page 12).

(see the instructions on page 12).

### WHAT YOU NEED

Thin card
Colored paper
Scissors
Ruler
Pencil
Glue

## CUTTING METHOD

**1** *Fold over a rectangle of card. Use a pencil and ruler to mark two equal lines at right angles to the central crease. Cut into these lines through both layers of card.*

**2** *Fold the section between the cuts over to the left and crease it. Then unfold it again and open up the card.*

**3** *Inside the card, lift up the section between the cuts so that it pops up and has a "mountain" fold instead of a "valley" fold.*

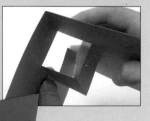

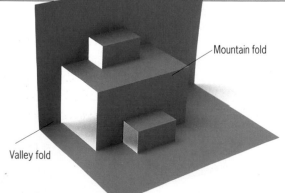

Mountain fold

Valley fold

▲ *Practice this simple method and then try cutting out different shaped lines to get different shaped pop-ups.*

198

◄ *If you stick the glued tabs far away from the central card crease, the pop-up shape will stretch flat when you open the card.*
*If you stick the glued tabs near to the central card crease, the pop-up shape will point outwards when you open the card.*

Central card crease

► *Try making more than one shape pop-up in the same card.*
*Make one pop-up shape come out of another. Cut out the big shape first, then the little shape.*

## GLUEING METHOD

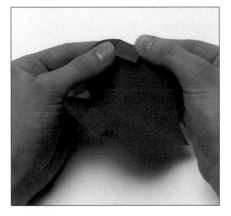

1 Fold round a rectangle of card. Decide what shape you want to pop out. It needs to be symmetrical (the same shape on both sides). Draw this shape on a separate piece of colored paper or card and add a tab to each side.

2 Cut out the shape and fold it in two, making a sharp crease along the middle. Fold the tabs to the back. Then unfold the shape and lay it flat. Run glue down the front of each tab and fold the shape round again (glued tabs outwards).

3 Open the card and lay the pop-up shape down on one side so that a glued tab sticks to the inside of the card. Close the card and press on it so that the other tab will stick to the inside. When you open your card the shape will pop up!

# Cards for fun

P OP-UPS ARE NOT THE ONLY WAY TO make cards exciting. The cards here are fun to make and also fun to receive. You can make the messages and pictures in them special for the people you are giving them to.

## ENTER THE SECRET DOORS!

You've really got to search for the secrets inside this card, because it's got doors within doors! You could write a secret message in the final section, or write "Open the birthday doors" on the front and someone's new age deep inside. You could write coded messages on all the doors, and the key to the code inside the last one.

**1** *Fold the paper in half widthwise. Fold it in half lengthwise, with a valley fold, then in half again, with a mountain fold.*

**2** *Draw a large door on the top sheet. Cut it out and fold it back — make sure you only cut through one layer of paper. Draw two smaller doors inside and do the same. Each time you open a door, draw and cut out another smaller opening on the sheet beneath.*

**3** *When you reach the last sheet, stop cutting. Unfold the card carefully to dab a little glue on the corners of each sheet to keep the doors shut. Then fold up the card once more and press down on it firmly to make it stick together.*

▲ *Your finished card can have as many doors as you have folded layers. When you have practiced, try making the doors different shapes.*

## CASTLE CARD

Lots of little opening doors and windows reveal hidden faces in this pop-up card. You could put members of your family in the windows — or your pets!

▶ *To make this special card, draw a castle or your own house, cut out flaps for windows, and stick the page onto a piece of backing card. Then draw or paint pictures in the windows.*

## WHIRLING WHEEL

Fix these wheels to the front of a card and write "Happy Birthday" on it. It is based on a traditional card design of over a hundred years ago, when novelty cards of all kinds were very popular.

Turn the wheels to get weird animal combinations!

**1** *Fold the card rectangle in half. Open it out again, with the fold pointing toward you as a mountain fold. Measure and mark the middle point on the right side. Use sharp scissors or a punch to make a hole.*

**2** *Cut out three card circles — small, medium, and big. Make a hole through the centre of each one. With the smallest one on top, push a paper fastener through each hole and through the middle of the card.*

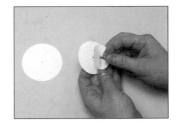

**3** *Open out the paper fastener inside the card — not too tightly or the wheels won't move round. Draw over the card and the circles. Turn the circles round to get different effects.*

◀ *On this card we have drawn animals (you could add the message "Have a wild birthday!"). You could draw human faces on differently decorated presents ("From all your friends"), or monsters ("Have a monster-ous birthday!").*

# Poster cards

Cards don't have to be small! You can fold thick paper or thin card many times to make a card that opens out to be huge! With a beautiful drawing on it, your friends will want to display it like a poster.

## UNFOLD A SURPRISE!

This card opens out into a big poster for an important, heartfelt message! It relies on careful measuring, scoring, and accurate folding. Try folding some scrap paper first to get the method right before you use more expensive materials.

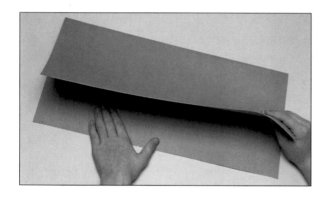

1 *Take the paper square. Score and make a mountain fold down the center. Then unfold the paper again.*

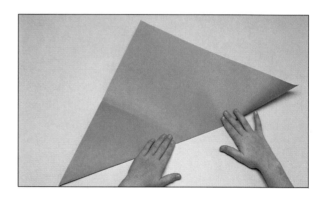

2 *Fold diagonally across opposite corners of the paper square to make two valley folds in the shape of an X.*

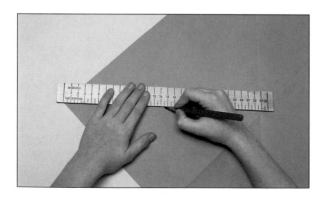

3 *Measure 5.75 inches in along the diagonal fold lines, coming from each corner. Mark each spot lightly with a pencil.*

4 *Use a set square to score a line from this point to the edges of the paper at right angles to the point. Do this on all four corners.*

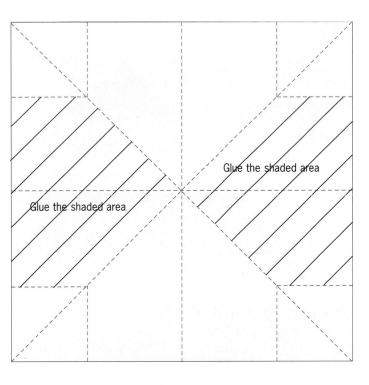

◄ *Glue the back of your folded piece of paper in the areas shown in this diagram. Then stick it onto the folded card rectangle (shown in step 6 below).*

Glue the shaded area

Glue the shaded area

▼ *Draw a big picture on the paper, or write a special message, so it surprises whoever opens it.*

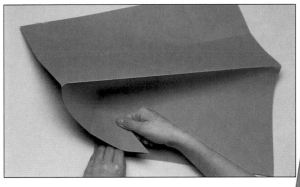

5 *Pinch up the corner between the straight lines you have made to change the diagonal valley fold to a mountain fold. Do this on all four corners.*

6 *Now fold and unfold the card rectangle in half. Press the paper down onto it, lining up the edges and center fold. When you shut your card, make sure the top and bottom of the paper and the corner pieces fold inward.*

# Paper collages

IF YOU TAKE A LOOK ROUND A greetings card shop, you might see cards that show unusual designs built up from scraps of thin paper, paint, and pieces of typing. This technique is called collage, and you can use it for lots of different effects. A favorite finished collage can be photocopied in color as many times as you like.

▶ *Write or draw on top of the collage paper.*

---

### STRETCHING PAPER

You can make pictures like the ones shown here on a background of card or thick paper. Because glue makes the background quite wet, if you use thin paper you need to stretch it before you use it — that way it will dry flat and smooth, without lumps and bumps. You don't need to stretch card.

#### WHAT YOU NEED

*White watercolor paper*
*Bowl of water*
*Brown paper masking tape*
*(available from stationery or craft shops)*

I Soak the sheet of paper in water for about ten minutes. Lift it out carefully and place it on a flat, clean board. Tape the edges to the board with brown paper masking tape. Wet the back of the masking tape to make it sticky. When dry, the paper can be used for the collage effects shown here. Keep it on the board while you work.

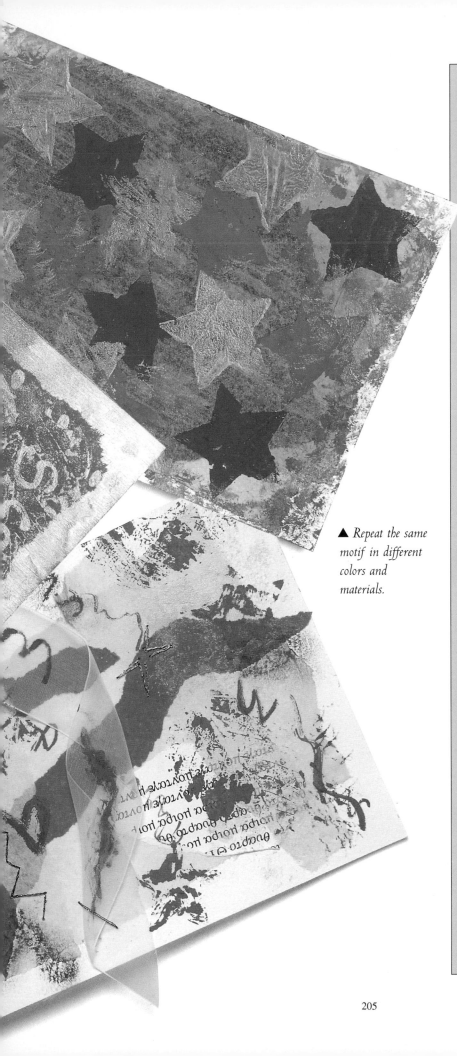

▲ *Repeat the same motif in different colors and materials.*

## TISSUE EXPERIMENTS

Tissue paper is good for making layered pictures because you can partly see through it to the other colors and patterns beneath. Sandwich it with pieces of type, or paint images or words on top. Thick tissue paper is easier to glue down than thin tissue.

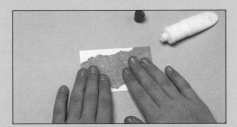

1 *Paint a thin layer of PVA glue over the back of each tissue piece. Lay the pieces down flat in the position you want.*

2 *Decorate the tissue by painting patterns or words on top.*

3 *Sew stitches through or try rubbing pastel or wax crayons over the top. Aim for an interesting texture and mix of colors. Words or painted images can give your work a theme, or you can simply use them to get an interesting abstract design.*

# Collage frames and mosaics

IT'S POSSIBLE TO DECORATE ALL kinds of objects using paper collage pieces. Think carefully about the colors of the pieces you choose to put together. Lay them out on paper first to get the arrangement right. You can glue on other objects, too, such as favorite shells, beads, or autumn leaves. The fun of collages is in experimenting!

## DECORATIVE MIRROR

You can use collage to decorate wood. You can make a mirror for your room into a work of art by decorating a plaque around a mirror tile with a favorite theme.

1 *Begin by planning your design and cutting out the paper pieces you want. Rub down the wood with fine sandpaper and then coat it with PVA glue.*

2 *Lay the paper pieces in place, concentrating on the areas that will show round the mirror tile. If they are small it is easier to place them with the end of a paintbrush.*

3 *Apply another coat of PVA over the top, and leave it to dry overnight. Then add another coat and, when this is dry, add a coat of varnish. Last, glue on the mirror tile.*

## PAPER MOSAIC

In Roman times, mosaics were made from tiny pieces of glass called *tesserae*. You can recreate this look by using paper pieces mounted on thick card or foamboard (a type of card with foam sandwiched in the middle). If you like, work your initials into the design.

1 *Before you start on a complicated picture, plan it out first. On a piece of graph paper, color in squares with crayons or felt-tips. This will give you an idea of what the finished mosaic will look like.*

2 *Glue colored paper to foamboard and use your craft knife to cut it evenly into lots of small squares.*

3 *Mix the filler with water to make a thick paste. Spread it, a little at a time, on a square of foamboard. Press the colored squares into the filler, leaving a gap between each one. Leave the mosaic to dry overnight. Coat it with a layer of watered-down PVA and, when this is dry, varnish it.*

▼ *Make a sea-horse for your mirror by cutting out a stencil and laying it on the mirror. Brush a thin layer of glue over the stencil, and remove it. Then scatter glitter over the glued area.*

# Paper weaving

WEAVING IS ONE OF THE SIMPLEST ways to use paper in a decorative way. Weave one color into a contrasting color that shows up well against it. You can use as many different colors as you like. Try weaving different paper textures together, too.

▼ *Cut each slit slightly longer than the last to make this corner weaving. It works well on both sides of the paper.*

### WHAT YOU NEED

Colored paper
Ruler
Scissors or craft knife

▶ *If you weave into the back of a ready-made envelope, make sure you avoid the glue strip intended for sticking the flap down.*

## BASIC WEAVING

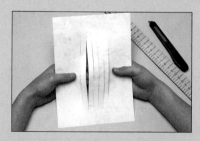

*1 Using a ruler and pencil, lightly draw in a number of vertical cutting lines, evenly spaced. Use a craft knife and ruler to cut along these lines to make slits.*

*2 Cut strips of colored paper, of equal lengths and wide enough for your design. Dab glue on one end of a strip and secure it to the back of your weaving. Feed it through the slits and secure the other end to the back with glue.*

*3 Weave all your strips in side by side. If you are weaving through thin paper, you may need to anchor it down as you go. Dab a few spots of glue under the sections between the slits, and flatten them down onto the weaving as you go along.*

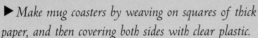

## CURVES AND ZIGZAGS

You needn't be restricted to straight slits. Try cutting them as zigzags or curves. Cut the weaving strips with irregular edges and use black on white or clashing colors

▶ *Make mug coasters by weaving on squares of thick paper, and then covering both sides with clear plastic.*

## HANGING HEART

Make this heart to hang on a Christmas tree or as a Valentine's Day gift.

**1** *Fold one square in half. Draw half a heart on it and cut round the shape to the fold. Do the same on the other square so you have two hearts.*

**2** *On each heart use a craft knife and ruler to cut slits going across. These should be .5 inch apart; do not make them go too near the edge.*

**3** *Weave the colored strips through the hearts, starting in the center and working out to the edge. Trim the strips to fit the hearts and glue them in place. Leave both hearts to dry.*

**4** *Glue the remaining strip in a loop to the back of one heart. Then glue the two hearts together back to back, hiding the bottom of the loop.*

### WHAT YOU NEED

Two 4-inch squares of thick paper

Craft knife, ruler, and pencil

Several contrasting-color paper strips 0.5 inch wide and at least 2 .75 inches long.

Glue and glue brush

Colored strip 0.5 inch wide and 4 .75 inches long

▼ *If you like, leave the top of the heart open. You could slip a message inside it. Or use it as a small bag for a wrapped chocolate to give to guests at the end of a meal or a party.*

# Woven baskets

Paper weaving techniques can be applied to 3D objects such as these woven baskets. They are perfect for holding and displaying Easter eggs. Try experimenting by weaving different paper textures to create unusual and eye-catching effects.

### WHAT YOU NEED

Different colored pieces of medium-thick paper — you could use ordinary or shiny gift-wrap paper
Ruler, scissors, and pencil
Glue and glue brush
Craft knife and cutting mat

## MINI-BASKET

Make mini-baskets and fill them with small Easter eggs in spring, chocolate money at Christmas, or a special present at any time.

1 *Choose a colored sheet of paper for the main part of the basket. Measure and draw the diagram opposite and cut the shape out. Then measure and draw a margin 0.5 inch inside, all the way round (shown as a grey line).*

2 *Measure, mark, and cut slits 0.5 inch apart down the center panel (shown as blue lines on the diagram on the next page). Do the same on the side panels (shown as red lines on the diagram). Cut carefully along all these slits.*

3 *Cut out lots of 0.5-inch-wide strips for weaving, some long enough for the center panel; some shorter for the side panels. When you have woven them in, glue down the ends.*

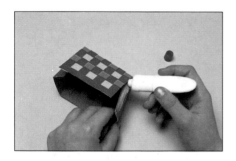

4 *On the wrong side of the basket, score along all the fold lines. Then fold the center panel round and fold the side panels up to meet it. Glue all the flaps inside the basket and leave it to dry.*

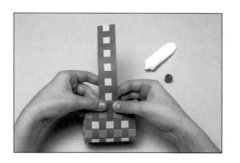

5 *Cut a strip of paper 1 x 4 .75 inches. Make 0.5-inch-wide slits across it, spacing them 0.5 inch apart. Weave a 0.5-inch-wide strip through the slits to make the basket handle. Glue the ends of the basket handle into the basket.*

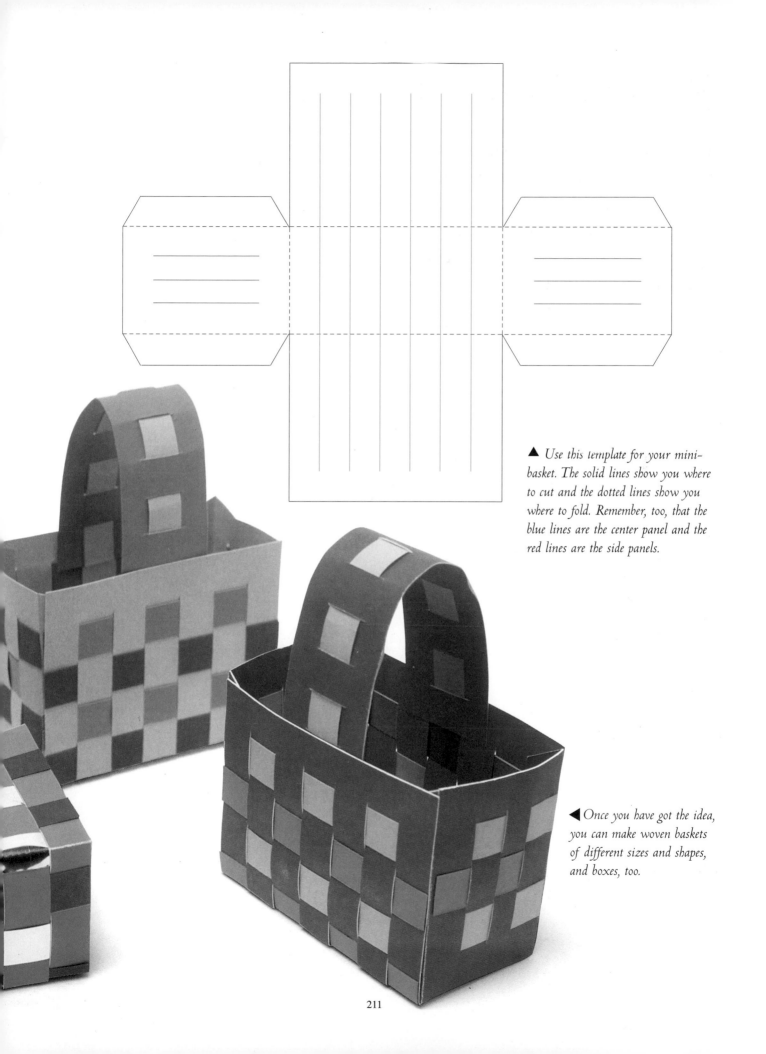

▲ Use this template for your mini-basket. The solid lines show you where to cut and the dotted lines show you where to fold. Remember, too, that the blue lines are the center panel and the red lines are the side panels.

◀ Once you have got the idea, you can make woven baskets of different sizes and shapes, and boxes, too.

# Perfect pricking

PRICKING IS A TRADITIONAL papercraft in the New England area of the United States. You do it by pricking a series of small holes through paper, then hanging the paper up so that the light shines through the holes from behind, bringing out the pattern.

## PRICKING PICTURES

It's best to choose a simple picture or pattern outline to prick. Very detailed, closely worked pricking is hard to see as the holes merge together. You can vary the size of the holes by using needles of different thicknesses. The larger the hole, the more light will shine through.

## SAILING BOAT

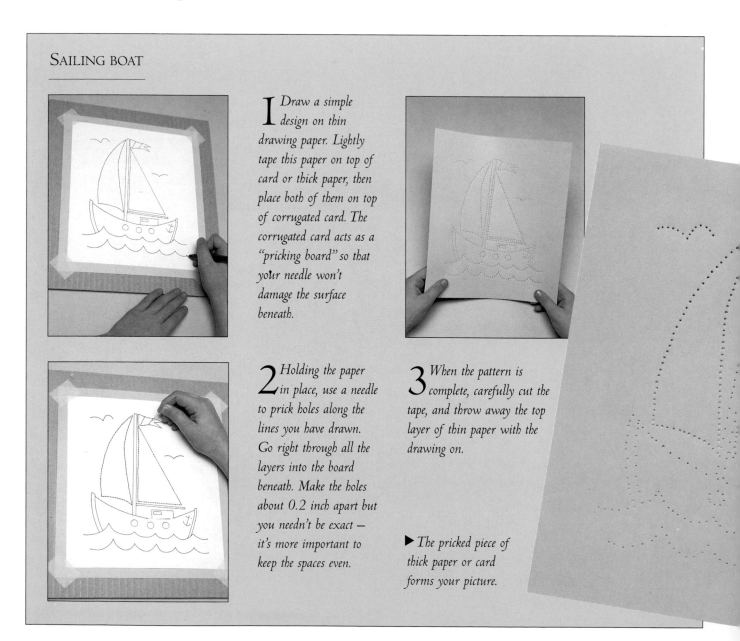

**1** Draw a simple design on thin drawing paper. Lightly tape this paper on top of card or thick paper, then place both of them on top of corrugated card. The corrugated card acts as a "pricking board" so that your needle won't damage the surface beneath.

**2** Holding the paper in place, use a needle to prick holes along the lines you have drawn. Go right through all the layers into the board beneath. Make the holes about 0.2 inch apart but you needn't be exact — it's more important to keep the spaces even.

**3** When the pattern is complete, carefully cut the tape, and throw away the top layer of thin paper with the drawing on.

▶ The pricked piece of thick paper or card forms your picture.

## PRICKED FRAME

Why not make a pricked frame, and place your pricked picture inside it? You can make the pattern on the frame pick up the theme of the picture.

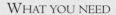

### WHAT YOU NEED

Thin card or thick paper, cut to size
Thin drawing paper for the pattern, cut to size
Pencil, sticky tape, and scissors
Set of different-sized sewing needles
Scrap piece of corrugated card
Colored tissue paper (optional)

I *Make a frame, following the instructions on page 19. In this example, the design reflects the sailing boat theme of the main picture.*

▼ *If you glue tissue paper of different colors behind the holes, the light will shine through making lines of different colors.*

2 *Tape your pricked picture behind the frame, but do not add any backing card. Hang it in a window or in front of a lamp, so that the light shines through the holes.*

# Toys and games

**I**N MANY PARTS OF THE WORLD PEOPLE make their own toys and games out of whatever there is to hand. You can do the same using paper and card. It is a lot cheaper than a visit to the toy shop and it provides two activities for the price of one: first you get to make the toy, then you get to play with it!

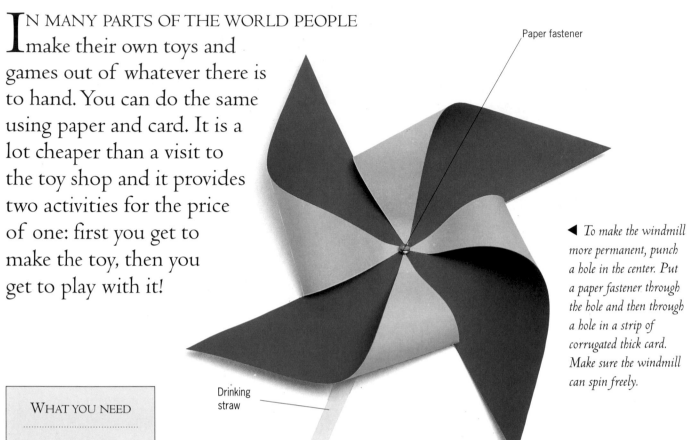

Paper fastener

Drinking straw

◀ *To make the windmill more permanent, punch a hole in the center. Put a paper fastener through the hole and then through a hole in a strip of corrugated thick card. Make sure the windmill can spin freely.*

## WHAT YOU NEED

Two squares of
sticky-back paper
in contrasting colors
Glue and glue brush
Scissors
Ruler
Drinking straw
Drawing pin

## WHIRLY WINDMILL

**1** *Stick the two pieces of paper back to back, lining up the edges. Fold the square diagonally to make crease marks in the shape of an X. Measure and cut along each crease from the corner halfway to the center.*

**2** *Fold and glue every other point into the center (they will overlap). Push the pin through the center and into the top of the straw. Blow to make the windmill spin round or put it outside for the wind to turn.*

# To Play Chancer

Ask a friend to choose a color from the top of the chancer. Use your fingers to "click" the chancer in and out, one click for each letter of the color your friend has chosen. Then show your friend the inside of the chancer and ask them to choose one of the numbers they can see. Use your fingers to click the chancer that number of times. After they choose another number, look beneath it and read out what you have written underneath. You could write forfeits, and then your friends must do them!

**1** *Fold the square along its diagonals to make a cross. Then flatten it out again.*

**3** *Turn the square over and again fold the corners to the center, making the creases sharp.*

**2** *Take each corner in turn and fold it to the center. Make every fold a sharp crease.*

**4** *Fold the square in half. Then open this fold and fold the square the other way.*

**5** *Put your thumbs and index fingers under the flaps and ease out the paper. Paint the outer flaps in different colors. Open it up and write numbers inside, up to eight. Write a message underneath each number.*

You may be able to move the chancer with one hand, but two is easier!

▶ *You could put nice messages inside the chancer, such as "You are beautiful," or rude ones, such as "You are ugly," or strange ones, such as "You have webbed feet."*

# Party table

Paper decorations are great for parties or festivals. They're inexpensive, and you can enjoy making them. Don't make the patterns too complicated, though, or put in lots of fussy details. Keep the ideas simple and you will achieve a more striking finished look.

## Napkin folding

Starched linen napkins are really good for holding their shape. They can be folded into very complicated patterns. Here are two simple folded shapes that will work just as well even with paper napkins. Run your finger along all the folds to make the creases sharp.

1 Unfold a napkin and lay it flat. Fold it diagonally to make a triangle. Fold the outer corners up the middle to make a square.

2 Turn the napkin over. Hold the top point in place, and fold it down to make a triangle.

3 Bend the triangle round and, at the back, tuck one corner inside the folds of the other. Stand the napkin up and gently bend the two loose flaps outwards.

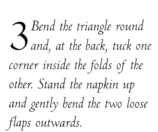

## Napkin for glass

1 Lay a napkin on the table, folded as a square — a paper one will be already folded this way. Fold the left corner over to the right.

▲ Put the napkin in a glass or a paper cup. Gently fan out the edges.

2 Take the right corner and fold half the napkin back to the center. Turn the napkin over, and fold the left corner back to the center. Fold the other corners to the center.

## TABLE ACCESSORIES

Start with a plain paper tablecloth and napkins, and stencil designs on them for your own unique theme. Then repeat the image on napkin rings, and place settings made from rectangles or round circles of card. You could even use the same stencil for your party invitations, too.

*1 Draw a design onto the stencilling card and cut round it carefully, using a craft knife. Keep the design simple so that you can cut it accurately.*

*2 Place the stencil on a napkin. Load your brush or sponge with a little paint or oil-based crayon. Then dab it through the stencil onto the napkin. When the paint is dry, gently lift off the card so that you can use it again.*

▲ *Use your stencil to decorate a whole range of party goods with a unified theme. You can vary the colors on different things.*

### NAPKIN RINGS

Make napkin rings to carry through your party table theme. Start with basic rings and decorate them by sticking on objects or paper shapes. You could even glue on small origami shapes (see pages 84–87).

*1 First decorate the strip by shaping the edges with scissors, painting it, or sticking colored paper onto it. Curve the strip round, and glue or tape it at the back to make a ring.*

# Party decorations

WHAT YOU NEED

Rectangles of thin card 8 x 5 inches
Small scissors or craft knife
Paints, crayons, and colored paper scraps

WHETHER YOU ARE HAVING A FEW friends round informally, or doing something a bit more special, individually made decorations will make your party really swing!

## TEDDY-IN-THE BOX SETTING CARDS

Make each guest a personalized table setting card that will follow your overall theme. Here are two ideas that you can easily adapt to make new images.

Write the name of each guest on the front of the cards.

Teddy pops up

**1** *Score and fold a card rectangle in half across the narrow middle. Lay it flat again and draw a teddy shape coming up from the middle line made by the fold.*

**2** *Decorate the teddy and the "box" beneath him. Carefully cut round the teddy shape above the card. Then fold the card back down again so the teddy stands up.*

## DINNER DRESS CARD

**1** *Score and fold a card rectangle in half across the narrow middle. Decorate each card with a white shirt and collar.*

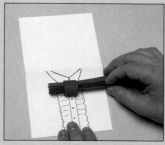

**2** *Glue a loop of colored paper near the top of the shirt. Make fan folds out of a strip of colored paper. Feed the folded paper through the loop.*

# PARTY PAPER CHAINS

Decorate the party room with your own unique paper chains. Here are a few ideas to try.

---

### WHAT YOU NEED

Colored string or cord
Colored tissue paper rectangles
for bow chain
Colored thin paper strips for cut-out chain

## CUT-OUT CHAIN

**1** *Fold a strip of paper back and forth concertina-style (see pages 12–14). Draw a shape on the front, making sure that the shape runs over both edges of the paper.*

**2** *Cut round the shape through all the paper layers. Do not cut along any folds. This is so that all the individual shapes are still joined when the chain is opened.*

**3** *When the strip is opened up, it makes a chain. If you want, join several chains together.*

▶ *Do not cut over the folds when you are cutting out the shapes or the banner will come apart. Try making them from different kinds of paper for different effects. Shiny paper chains looks great swinging from the walls and ceiling!*

You could stick lots of different colored chains together to make one long one

▶ *To make a chain of bows, put a length of colored string round the middle of bunched-up rectangles of tissue paper. Fan out the rectangles to look like bows.*

# Boxes and bags

A HANDMADE BOX OR BAG IS AN ideal way to make a gift extra-special. Use thick, flexible paper to make a bag, and find thin, bendy card to make a box. Decorate your gift containers in themes related to the present inside.

## GIFT BASKET BOX

Here's an easy way to make a gift container using paper, and the method has the added benefit of recycling old packaging, too!

*1 Use a ruler and felt-tip to measure up from the bottom of the drinks bottle. Mark a line round the bottle as high as you want your bag to be, and cut round it.*

*2 Measure the base of the bottle, and up from the base. Cut a strip of card or paper about 1 inch higher and 1 inch longer than the container.*

*3 Put glue round the outside of the container and along one narrow edge of the paper strip. Wrap the strip round the container and glue the overlapping edge firmly at the back.*

*4 Put some crumpled tissue or cellophane in the bottom to cushion your gift, and more round it to cover it up. Then tie a pretty ribbon round the whole box.*

## BASIC BAG

Once you've made a gift bag, wrap your present loosely in tissue and put it inside. This template shows measurements for a medium-sized bag. If you want a bigger or smaller one, make sure you alter all the dimensions equally.

**1** *Use a pencil and ruler to draw this bag design on the back of the paper. Score lightly along all the black dotted lines. Fold inwards all the lines you have scored.*

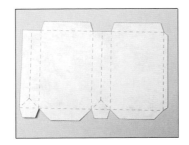

**2** *Turn over and score along the red dotted lines. Fold them in and then flatten them again. Then turn over again and glue down the tabs along the top edge (this makes the bag extra-strong).*

**3** *Glue together the tabs underneath. Then glue the side of the bag together and hold it until it dries. Gently pinch the sides of the bag along the lines you scored and folded.*

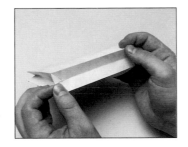

**4** *Pinch the top of the bag together, and punch through it to make two sets of holes on either side. Thread a length of ribbon through each set of holes, and knot the ends inside the bag.*

This bag is decorated with collage strips to match the ribbon handles

# Storage boxes

A STURDY BOX WITH A LID MAKES an ideal toy box or container for a collection. It can be made in any size using a simple template, and decorated to suit its contents. A decorated box is also an ideal way to present a gift to someone.

## BOX WITH LID

Here is a simple box with its own separate lid. You can make several smaller ones to fit inside.

1 *Score along the lines. Fold them all inward and then flatten them out again. Fold the box up as shown.*

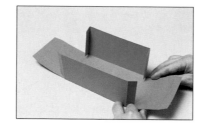

2 *Dab glue along the narrow side edges, and fold the box up again. Hold the edges together firmly while the glue dries.*

3 *Brush glue along the inside of the two top narrow edges. Fold them to the inside, and hold them in place until the glue dries.*

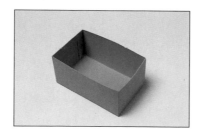

Cut along the solid lines; fold along the broken lines.

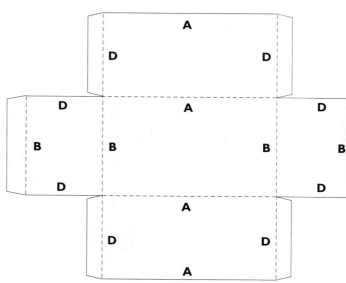

▲ *To make the box, copy template A onto the back of the card. Make it any overall size you like, but make sure that measurements that have the same letter are the same as each other.*

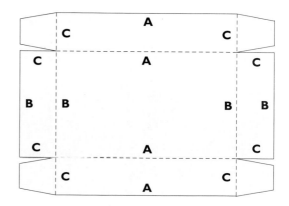

▲ *To make the lid, use template B. Fold up and glue the lid in the same way as the box. Wait until it is dry before you put it on your box.*

◀ To give your box a frill, cut strips of crepe paper twice the depth of the lid. Paste glue round the inside of the lid and press the crepe paper onto it, gathering up the crepe paper into pleats as you do so.

▶ This box has two more boxes inside, each one made slightly smaller than the last. They all match, and open up a bit like a set of Russian dolls.

◀ This box was made out of card with a pattern cut in the sides before it was folded up. Contrasting colored paper was stuck on the inside edges so it shows through the holes.

# Papier mache molds

Papier mache is a great way to recycle paper. Newspaper, computer printout paper, cartridge paper, and even tissue and crepe paper are all suitable. There are several different methods. Start with layering and, if you enjoy this, go on to work with pulp.

## WHAT YOU NEED

Balloon and thread
Bowl (for mixing)
Wallpaper paste (containing a fungicide), mixed with water to a creamy consistency
Paper torn up into small squares
Paintbrushes
Apron and newspaper (to protect clothes and table)
Craft knife or sharp scissors
White water-based paint
Paints to decorate

## LAYERING A BALLOON MASK

Laying strips of paper on top of each other around a mold makes a strong paper crust. The most important rule is to let the paper dry between layers, and so this method takes a few days to complete. The steps below show how to make a mask using a balloon as a mold.

*1 Hang up the balloon with the thread. Soak paper squares in the paste, then lay them overlapping on the balloon until it is covered. Immediately add a second layer.*

*2 Let the pasted paper dry for several hours. Then add two more layers, and let it dry again. Put on six to eight layers in total, letting it dry every two layers.*

*▶ When the undercoat is dry, decorate your mask, making holes for the eyes and mouth. Then varnish it two or three times to protect it.*

*3 Pop the balloon by sticking a long needle right through the paper. Then cut the shape in half to make an oval. Paint it with white water-based paint, and let it dry.*

*▶ This "fire" mask was made by cutting out a card template (see page 74) with the top cut to look like flames. You can then use layers of papier mâché to alter the surface texture of the mask — for example, to give a raised outline to the eye holes and the outside edge.*

224

## Making a Bowl

You can layer papier mache onto lots of different molds, and they needn't cost anything. Here we show you how to make a bowl using another bowl as a mold. To remove the mold easily after your work is dry, before applying the papier mache either cover the mold with a layer of petroleum jelly, or wrap it in a smooth layer of plastic film.

### What You Need

Paper squares of colored tissue paper
Wallpaper paste or thinned PVA glue
Shape for mold
Petroleum jelly or plastic film
Scissors and sandpaper
Paintbrushes
Undercoat, paint, and varnish

**1** *Soak the paper squares in the paste, and cover the mold with petroleum jelly or plastic film. Lay the paper over the mold until it is covered.*

**2** *When the mold is completely covered, paint a thick layer of thinned wallpaper paste or PVA all over it. Repeat with more paper and glue twice more. Leave the mold to dry for 24 hours in a warm place.*

**3** *Remove the papier mâché shape carefully from the mold. Trim any rough edges carefully with scissors. Then rub it gently all over with fine sandpaper to smooth it, and paint it with undercoat.*

**4** *Cut a piece of decorative colored paper to fit the bottom of the bowl. Paint a thin layer of paste in the bottom of the bowl, and press the paper onto it gently. Cut circles of colored tissue paper to decorate the sides.*

**5** *When the decorations are finished and completely dry, paint two or three layers of varnish over the entire bowl, inside and outside, to protect it.*

Choose the colors for decorating your bowl to fit in with what you plan to put in it.

# Papier mache models

Once you have made a few papier mache items using simple molds that you remove, try following the steps here to make more complicated things, such as animals. First you have to make the basic shape, called an armature. Start with a simple one!

### WHAT YOU NEED

Cardboard tubes from toilet rolls and kitchen rolls, for the tail, neck, ears, and legs
Carboard oblong box with a lid, such as a shoe box
Smaller oblong box for the head
Scissors, glue, and sticky tape
Papier mâché for layering

## ANIMAL MODEL

In Japan, papier mache replicas of animals are thought to ward off evil spirits. Make your own by layering onto a cardboard body base, or armature. An armature, unlike a mold, is not removed when the model is dry.

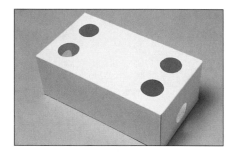

**1** *Plan out your animal armature before you start. Make holes in the main body box where you want to stick tubes in.*

**2** *To make the leg tubes, use a tube of paper and snip about 0.25 inch into one end, evenly all round with 0.25-inch gaps. Fan out these tabs. Measure four tubes so that you get the legs all the same length.*

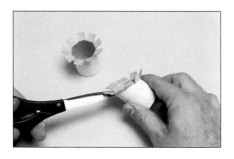

**3** *The tail tube needs to be at an angle. Snip into the tube deeper on one side, to make tabs that are longer on one side than on the other.*

**4** *Glue the tabs of the leg and tail tubes inside the holes on the main body. Then make more tubes for the neck, join it at an angle to a smaller box for the head, and add the ears.*

**5** *Once your animal body is constructed, layer papier mâché onto it. Add several layers for strength and let them dry completely.*

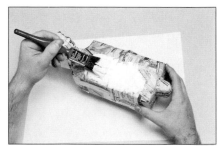

**6** *When your animal is quite dry, paint on a thick layer of undercoat. Afterwards, decorate it as you like, and finally varnish it. Handle it with care when you work.*

## PAPIER MACHE TEDDY BEAR

Once you have learned the simple technique of using an armature, you can apply it to a whole range of other animals, for example this teddy bear (see right). Create an armature for the teddy bear using toilet rolls for the body and limbs, and a ball or other round object for the head. Build up the ears using the layering technique.

▶ *Once the layers have dried, paint a beige base color over the entire bear. Use white for the feet and hands and then add the mouth and eye detail in black.*

Painted on eyes and nose

Studded collar

▲ *The dog collar is made from a thin strip of textured card, with gold studs made from round pieces of gold paper. You could make the studs raised by cutting a line from the edge to the center, overlapping one edge over the other, and sticking them to make a shallow cone (see page 25).*

# Stationery shop

STATIONERY DOESN'T HAVE TO BE BORING! HERE ARE some suggestions for making unusual envelopes and writing paper for special occasions. Try these two ways to make your very own stationery storage folders. They're ideal for keeping paper scraps and examples of artwork, too.

### WHAT YOU NEED

A big piece of stiff paper
or thin card

Glue and glue brush

Ruler and pencil

Scissors

Sticky tape

Length of tape

## LACE-UP WALLET

Use the template shown on the right to make a special wallet. You don't have to make it the size shown here, as long as all the sides that have the same letters are the same length. For example, all the sides marked A could be 20 inches and all those marked B could be 10 inches.

1 *Using a ruler, draw the wallet as shown in the diagram (far right). Cut out this shape and score the lines.*

2 *Cut holes where shown. Cut the edges into a wavy shape if you like. Fold in the left and right sides. Fold up the bottom edge, and glue it on top of the left and right sides.*

3 *Put a piece of sticky tape over each set of holes. Cut into the tape over each hole to make a cross shape. Use a pencil to push the tape through the hole and then fold the pieces round to the back.*

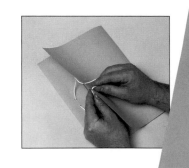

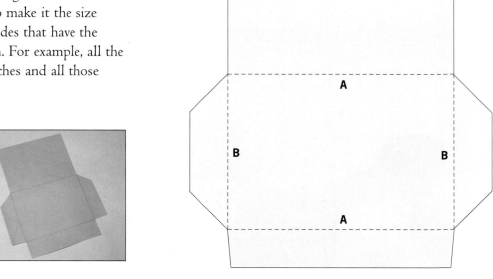

Cut along the solid lines; fold along the broken lines.

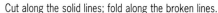

▼ *To close the wallet, lace the string through the bottom set of holes, then up through the top set. Tie a bow.*

## Two kinds of envelope

You can make good envelopes out of medium-thickness paper. Make them any size you like, by scaling the measurements shown here up or down. Score the lines and fold the envelopes as shown.

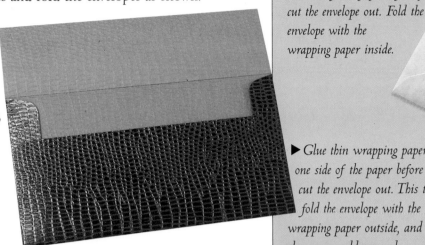

▶ *Envelope with a straight-edged flap.*

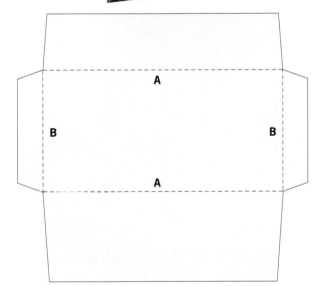

◀ *This envelope has a V-shaped flap.*

## Decorating envelopes

▶ Glue thin wrapping paper to one side of the paper before you cut the envelope out. Fold the envelope with the wrapping paper inside.

▶ Glue thin wrapping paper to one side of the paper before you cut the envelope out. This time, fold the envelope with the wrapping paper outside, and glue on an address and stamp label if you want to mail your work.

▶ Stick on torn pieces of brightly colored tissue paper to line a pre-made envelope. If you stick on pieces of cut paper, position them away from the fold line.

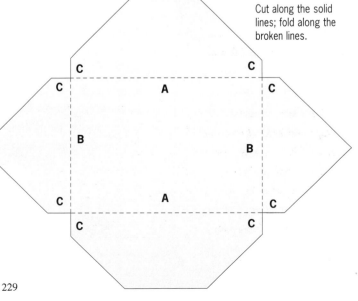

Cut along the solid lines; fold along the broken lines.

# Personal stationery

## WHAT YOU NEED
....................................
Writing paper
Sponge
Craft knife
Water-based paint
Kitchen paper

A S WELL AS MAKING YOUR OWN WRITING paper, cards, and envelopes, you can decorate them – or ready-bought stationery – in a way that makes them uniquely yours. Put your own initials on them, or add pictures special to you – showing your hobbies, perhaps, or illustrating something in your letter.

## PRINTING

1 *Make a printing block with a piece of thin sponge – look for thin, sponge-backed pan cleaners in the supermarket. Cut out a simple shape, such as the initial letter of your name.*

2 *Mix water-based paint on a flat plate – choose a pale color that you will be able to write over. Dab the sponge into the paint and then onto some kitchen paper to get rid of any excess. Then push it down onto the writing paper as often as you like.*

▼ *You can decorate just the margins of your paper, or all over it provided that the stamps are light enough for you to write over. Then you could make envelopes to match.*

Cut as many initial letters as you like – why not make decorated paper as presents for your friends?

# PICTURE TAB PAPER

Here's an easy but clever way to make an unusual letterhead for the top of a special letter. When the right-hand tab is pulled, a new picture appears! You could write words or draw pictures on the hidden part.

## WHAT YOU NEED

Two pieces of good-quality A4 writing paper

Strip of thick paper 8.25 x 0.75 inches

Craft knife

Ruler and pencil

Rubber

Felt-tips for decoration

Glue and glue brush

*1 Measure and draw two 1-inch long slits near the top of the paper as shown. Cut carefully along the slits with a craft knife.*

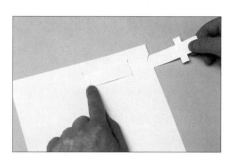

*2 Cut the thick paper into a strip with tabs, as shown. Thread it through the slits, with the end underneath.*

*3 Push the strip in as far as it will go. Draw a picture or write a message on the part of the strip that shows.*

*4 Pull the tab out a little and draw another picture on the new section that is revealed. Then push the tab back into position.*

▶ *You can make as many threaded strips as you like, but don't put them too close together or your writing paper may tear.*

231

# Tissue flowers

TISSUE PAPER IS TRANSLUCENT, WHICH means it is thin enough for light to shine through. That gives it a delicate, glowing quality that you can use to good effect in papercraft designs. It's cheap to buy and comes in lots of bright colors.

## TOPIARY FLOWER TREE

These flowers made from balls of tissue make a pretty table decoration. Use an air ball to anchor a small version, and a florist's oasis if you want to make a larger one — see the tip below for what these are.

1 *If you have an oasis, use a pencil to poke holes in it. Then push dowelling or the pencil up into the oasis or air ball. Cut a long strip of tissue and wrap it round the stick. Tape it in place at the top and bottom.*

2 *Cut out tissue circles about 5 inches in diameter. You can do this quickly by drawing round the edge of a plate as a template, and cutting through several layers together. Fold each circle in half, in half again and then in half again. Twist the end.*

3 *If you use an air ball, glue round the holes first. Then push a tissue piece into each hole. Fluff out the tissue to cover up the ball or oasis. Add more until the ball is covered.*

4 *Stick the dowelling or pencil firmly down into the flower pot of sand and tie some ribbon round the top for decoration.*

### ANCHORING THE FLOWER

An air ball (a practice golf ball) is made of plastic with holes in. An oasis (used by florists for flower arranging) is a type of spongy foam ideal for sticking delicate things in.

## TISSUE ROSES

Glue these roses onto hats, masks, fancy dress costumes, and gift boxes.

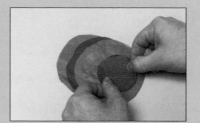

1 *Cut out two small tissue circles (use a cup as a template if you like). Cut out two medium-sized ones and two larger ones. Lay the circles on top of each other with the biggest at the bottom.*

2 *Twist them together underneath the center, so that they bunch together like petals, and gently spread them out. Wrap a small piece of tape around the twist to hold them in place.*

## PARTY STICKS

Make these party sticks out of brightly colored paper and strong straws. Stick them in ice-cream sundaes as decoration.

1 *Fold a sheet of tissue until it is about 3 inches wide, with about ten layers on top of each other; if it is pre-folded, don't unfold it. Cut a section 4 inches from the top.*

3 *Cut down into the tissue to make a fringe. Push your finger down into the middle to spread the fringe outwards.*

2 *Glue one edge of the section to the top of a stick, with about 2.5 inches poking up above the stick. Wind the tissue round and round. Glue the other edge in place.*

▶ *You can paint the stick, if you like. Make a collection to decorate your party table.*

# Puppets and kites

THERE'S NO END TO THE TOYS YOU CAN MAKE with paper. Here we show you how to make shadow puppets, and a clever kite that fills with air when you run with it. Try inventing your own shapes and patterns for both of these!

## SHADOW PUPPETS

Shadow puppets are traditional in parts of Asia. You can make your own versions in card and tissue paper with a screen to perform behind. Or you can simply hold your puppet up to a window or a lamp so that the light shines through it.

**1** *Draw a shape onto the card. Cut round the outline and cut out smaller shapes from the middle. Don't go too near the edge.*

**2** *Brush glue over the back of the animal. Stick tissue on so that it shows through the holes. Trim off any edges that show round the outside.*

**3** *To make a puppet screen, cut out one side of a cardboard box. Cut out the middle to make a frame. Tape a piece of greaseproof paper to the back over the hole.*

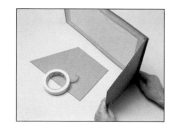

**4** *Cut two side pieces from the box, and tape them to the back of your screen as shown, to make it stand up. The tops of the supports should slope downwards.*

**5** *Place the screen near the edge of a table. Place a lamp behind the table, so it shines directly through the screen from behind. To perform with your puppets, tape or glue plant sticks to the backs so you can hold them from beneath. Sit your audience in front of the screen. Close the curtains and turn off all lights. Then switch on the lamp, and move your puppets behind the screen.*

# CARP KITE

Every year in Japan, there is a kite festival for children to fly their home-made carp kites. The carp fish traditionally represents strength. Make your own version and hang it up as a decoration when you're not flying it.

## WHAT YOU NEED

Different-colored tissue paper
Glue, scissors, pencil, and thin card
Needle and strong thread

1 *Cut out two carp shapes from tissue paper. You can use the big one on this page to help you. Stick on tissue eyes, body stripes, and fins.*

2 *Turn them over. Cut two strips of card 2 inches wide. Glue a strip along the edge of each mouth, on the wrong side. Trim the card to match the mouth edges. Leave them to dry thoroughly.*

3 *Run a very thin line of glue round the inside of one body shape but not along the mouth, which will stay open. Lay one fish body on top of the other and gently press along the glued edges. Leave them to dry.*

4 *Thread the needle with cotton and knot one end. Thread it out through the card in the middle of a mouth. Thread it round and back through the other mouth to make a loop. Or, if you prefer, tape the thread in place.*

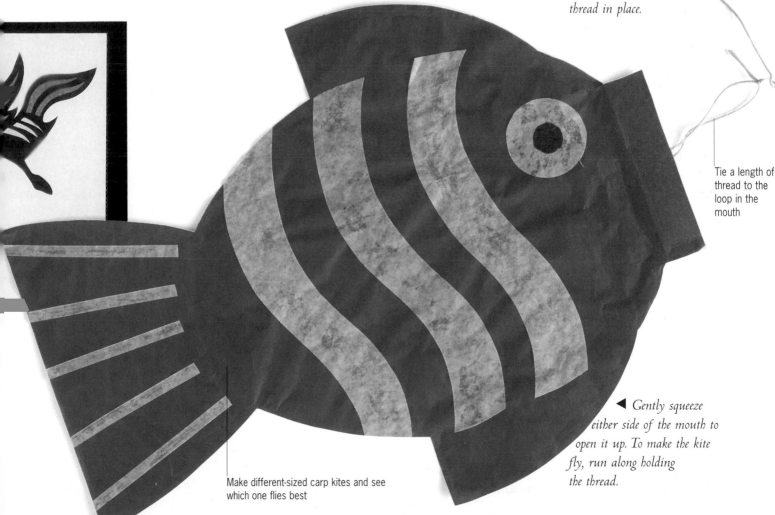

Tie a length of thread to the loop in the mouth

◄ *Gently squeeze either side of the mouth to open it up. To make the kite fly, run along holding the thread.*

Make different-sized carp kites and see which one flies best

# Handy hats

MAKE A FASHION HAT YOU CAN really wear, or a zany fancy-dress hat for wild parties. The hats on the right are made from basic paper shapes. They can be personalized by adding your own decorations.

## CONE HATS

A basic cone shape is very adaptable. By making a tall or a flattish cone, you can get different-looking hat designs.

### WHAT YOU NEED

Stiff paper or thin card, 36 x 20 inches for a tall hat
Scissors, sticky tape, and pencil
Material for decoration

Add a rim (see page 68) to make a wizard's hat

*1 Lay the paper rectangle on a flat surface. Starting at the bottom right corner, roll it up into a cone shape — the point will be in the top right corner.*

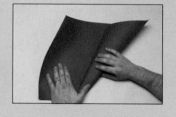

*2 Holding the cone together, try it on your head for size and adjust it until it fits. To hold the cone in place, tape along the loose edge on the outside and along the loose edge inside.*

*3 Draw a pencil line round the bottom of the cone to make a level edge — if you need to, use a ruler to get it even all round. Cut round the line.*

▶ *To make a princess' hat, attach strips of tissue paper or crepe paper to the pointed end of the hat.*

▶ *This party hat is made from a shorter, flatter cone decorated with paper scraps.*

## CHINESE HAT

This style of flat cone hat is traditional among workers in China. It is excellent for providing shade from the sun.

### WHAT YOU NEED

Piece of stiff paper or thin card, at least 20 x 20 inches
Something round to use as a template, with a diameter of 16–20 inches
Pencil, sticky tape, ruler
Materials for decoration
Cord or string

1 *Place the round shape on the paper and draw round it. Cut out the circle. Use a ruler to find the center of the circle. Draw a line from the center to the edge and cut along this line.*

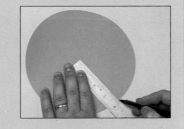

2 *Bring one edge round to overlap the other, to make a shallow cone. Tape the edges together. Tape two lengths of string opposite each other inside the hat. Tie them round your chin to keep the hat on.*

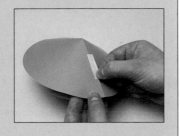

▼ *Make a hat from thin but strong paper. Thread wool through a large darning needle and sew it in big stitches round the bottom of the hat.*

Plaited ribbon

▶ *Chinese hats were popular fashion items in the 1950s. Get "the look" by adding a big tissue or crepe paper bow to the back of your hat (see page 72). Or spiral a piece of rope, curtain cord, or plaited ribbon down from the top.*

▶ *Roll up and twist lengths of crepe paper and glue them round a hat, spiralling down from the top.*

237

# Fancy dress hats

ONE SURE WAY TO GET YOURSELF noticed at a party is to wear a stunning hat of your own make. Adapt the examples shown here by coloring or decorating them.

### WHAT YOU NEED

Card and colored paper

Glue, scissors, and ruler

Pencil and compass

Sharp scissors

## HEADBAND HAT

You can make many hats that look very different by using simple paper headbands.

**1** *Cut a strip of card 2.5 inches wide and 3 inches longer than the measurement round your head. Put the two ends together, overlapping by 1.5 inches, check the fit and tape them together.*

**2** *Glue the band to the bottom of a hat – here, a silver band, decorated with scrunched-up sweet papers, is attached to a piece of gold card with spikes cut out of the top to make a crown.*

## RIMMED HAT

Add rims to top hats, cowboy hats – anything!

**1** *Make the top part of a hat (either a cone or a wide band). Lay it on top of another, bigger piece of card, and draw a wider circle around the base.*

**2** *Use a ruler to find and mark the center of the circle. With a pencil and compass, draw another circle about 1 inch inside the first one.*

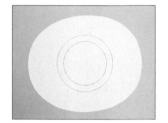

**3** *Cut round the inner circle. Snip from the inner edge to the line of the other circle to make tabs that you can push up. Put the hat top over the tabs, and glue the two together.*

▼ *Feather shapes from colored paper, glued to a decorated headband, make a Native American headdress.*

◄ *Two rabbit ears made of gray card with pink insides complete a rabbit headband.*

# SUN CAP

Make this basic sun-cap shape and personalize it by changing the brim.

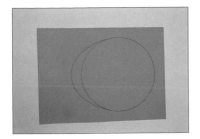

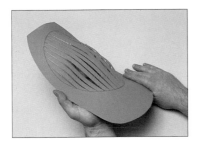

### WHAT YOU NEED

Piece of stiff paper 9.5 x 12.5 inches

Sharp scissors, or craft knife and cutting board

Pencil, ruler, and compass

Tape measure

**1** *Measure round your head and draw a circle this size at one end of the card rectangle. Using your pencil, make the circle into an oval as shown.*

**2** *Inside the oval, measure and draw lines 0.5 inches apart. Cut along the lines to the edge of the oval.*

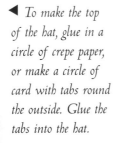

**3** *Round off the corners of the rectangle and push the oval partly down onto your head with the brim at the front. If the hat is too small, cut the lines a little longer towards the front.*

◀ *To make the top of the hat, glue in a circle of crepe paper, or make a circle of card with tabs round the outside. Glue the tabs into the hat.*

Glue on colored paper to decorate the brim

Cut round the edge of the cap to make a wiggly shape

239

# Fancy dress clothes

NEXT TIME YOU WANT A FANCY DRESS FOR a party, you won't need to hire an expensive costume — instead, you can make one of these outfits all on your own using papercraft skills. Ask your friends to help you, and it will be even more fun!

## TUBE DRESS

This basic crepe paper dress can be adapted for a variety of different looks.

*1 First take your measurements: round your bottom plus 6 inches for the width, and from under your arm to just above your knee for the length. Cut out a rectangle of crepe paper. Put glue down one edge and bring the two edges together to make a tube, overlapping the glued edge by 2 inches.*

*2 Wriggle into the tube. Get a friend to help you fit the narrow strips over your shoulders from front to back, to make straps. Get them to mark where the straps meet the front and back, and how long they should be. Then take off the tube and glue the straps in place.*

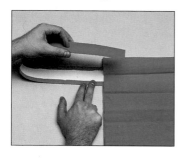

*3 Using different-colored crepe paper, cut some strips about 4 inches deep, and the same width as the tube. Cut almost up to the edge to make a fringe, then put glue along the uncut edge, and glue the fringe to the tube dress. Make as many fringes as you like.*

### WHAT YOU NEED

Rolls of different-colored crepe paper
Tape measure and pencil or felt-tip pen
Glue and gluebrush
Two colored paper strips 18 x 1.5 inches
Scissors

This headband is made from silver card with a feather shape and a big star.

A fringe has been added around the top of the dress.

◄ *This Native American dress is decorated with stars.*

The hem of the dress is fringed, and two contrasting fringes have also been added on.

240

## CAVEMAN OUTFIT

Cut a rectangle of brown crepe paper and, before making a tube dress, cut the top and bottom edges so they look ragged. Stick on some patches of colored paper and draw felt-tip stitching round these.

The club is made from a kitchen paper tube covered with brown crepe paper, with a rolled-up ball of crepe paper stuck on the end.

## TWENTIES DRESS

Make a short tube dress out of brightly colored paper, with a paper fringe on the hem in a contrasting color. Then add lots of squares of crepe paper, glued to the hem of the dress, to make an uneven hemline. You can even make a paper "boa" to complete your outfit (see right)!

## PAPER BOA

*Feather boas were worn by all the "flappers" in the Twenties. Here's an idea for one made out of paper.*

### WHAT YOU NEED

50 squares of crepe paper 12 x 12 inches, or a box of square tissues
Strong thread 39 inches long
Sewing needle

**I** *Lay each square flat and pick it up in the middle. It will fold into an arrow shape. Gently twist round the top.*

**2** *Thread the needle and make a knot in one end. Then thread through the top of each arrow shape. Push the paper down, so it bunches and sticks out in different directions.*

**3** *When you have finished, tie another knot in the end of the thread. Puff out the paper so the boa looks good.*

# Shirts and waistcoats

Here is some more wild and whacky paper clothing to try out. If you do it well, no one will guess what your stylish designer gear is really made of, but don't go out in the rain!

## Paper bow tie

Make bow ties as bright as you like! Wear them for fun with your ordinary clothes, or as part of fancy dress.

1 Cut a piece of crepe paper 6.25 x 13.75 inches. Fold the two ends in to the center. Glue or tape them down, with one edge overlapping the other.

2 Cut the elastic to the measurement of your neck plus 4.75 inches, and knot the two ends together. Scrunch up the middle of the tie and glue the knot to the back.

3 Cut a strip of paper 1.25 x 2.5 inches, and wrap it round the middle, taping it in place at the back. Fan out the tie on either side.

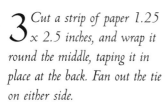

Decorate your tie with pieces of paper in a contrasting color

## Waistcoat

Make a fancy dress waistcoat to go with your tie! You could add a sheriff's badge for a cowboy waistcoat, or fancy buttons and a lace collar.

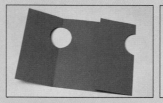

1 Cut the paper to your size. Fold the two ends into the middle. Cut out an arm circle on each fold 2 inches from the top.

2 Turn down the corners to make a collar. Pockets, buttons, or badges make good decorations for your waistcoat.

Badge

Fancy buttons

242

# FALSE SHIRT

Fool your friends with this fake shirt! Tie it round your neck and waist, and then button up a jacket or cardigan over the top so that nobody can see the edges.

## WHAT YOU NEED

Stiff paper
Ruler, pencil, and tape measure
Scissors
Four pieces of string, 12 inches long, knotted at one end
Hole punch
Colored paper pieces to glue on for decoration

**1** *Cut the paper into the shape using your body measurements. In the middle at the top cut out a curve for your neck.*

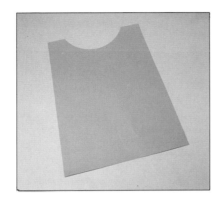

**2** *Round off the corners. Punch holes in the sides and the shoulders, and thread a length of string through each hole. Decorate your shirt however you like. Then tie the top strings behind your neck, and the bottom strings round your waist.*

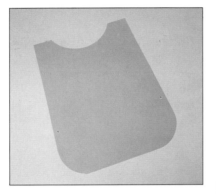

▲ *This fake dress shirt has a white paper collar, shirt frill, and black bow tie. The frill is made from a length of lace.*

◄ *This clown's shirt has a ruff made from a circle of crepe paper. Cut a line from the side to the middle and concertina-fold the circle. Then open it out and glue the edges to the shirt. Decorate the shirt with paper shapes.*

243

# Mask magic

$M$ASKS ARE THE PERFECT WAY to dress up a party costume, and you can really let your imagination go. Better still, invite your friends round for a mask-making day – provide materials such as glue and card, and you can all make your own unique masks!

WHAT YOU NEED

Scrap paper and stiff paper or thin card
Scissors, pencil, and tape measure
Glue and glue brush
Stiff straw, plant stick, or length of elastic
Paint or paper pieces for decoration

## EYE MASK

This is one of the easiest masks to make, so it's probably a good one to start with. You can decorate it in lots of different ways.

*1* *Practice first by cutting a rectangle of scrap paper 7 x 3 inches. Fold it in half to make a shape 3.5 x 3 inches. On one side draw a round shape up to the fold.*

*2* *Cut out the outline shape. Then unfold the paper, and hold it up to your face to check the size. Mark where the eyes should be, and cut them out.*

*3* *Once you are happy with the size and eye positions on your practice mask, use it as a template to cut out a mask from stiff paper. Decorate this with paints or glued-on paper shapes.*

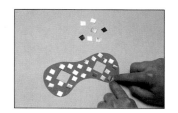

*4* *Punch a hole in each side, thread some elastic through, and tie the mask round your head. Alternately, tape a stick to one side, so that you can hold the mask up to your eyes.*

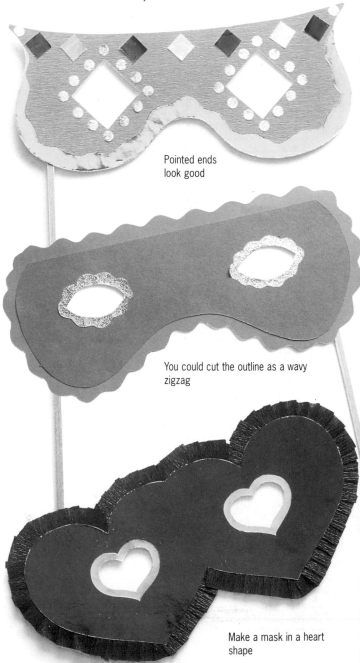

Pointed ends look good

You could cut the outline as a wavy zigzag

Make a mask in a heart shape

▲ *Make eye masks more elaborate by glueing on card hats and hair. Paint the eye mask skin color and draw eyebrows and eyelashes on.*

## VENETIAN FIREBIRD MASK

This traditional design is worn at the spring carnival in Venice that takes place every year in the week of Mardi Gras.

**1** *Fold the card triangle in half lengthwise. Fold back two corners on the nose section of your eye mask.*

▼ *For an authentic Venetian mask, stick three or four layers of papier mâché pieces over the card before you paint it (see page 54). You could pinch up the papier mache to make a raised edge around the eyes.*

**2** *Put the nose over the eye mask, and tape or glue the two corners inside the nose to keep it in place.*

# More amazing masks

**M**ASKS ARE POPULAR THE WORLD OVER AT festivals and celebration times. Look in the library for books on different countries to get some extra ideas for decorating the basic masks shown here.

### FULL FACE MASKS

This mask covers your whole face. You can adapt it to any theme you like.

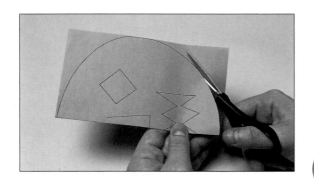

**1** *Fold the paper in half lengthwise. Draw half an oval, an eye, half a mouth, and half a nose shape. Cut round the shapes you have drawn and open up your mask.*

**2** *Punch a hole on either side, just above where your ears will be. Knot elastic or string lengths through the holes so you can tie them round your head.*

▲ *This Neptune mask has different lengths of green and blue paper making a beard and hair. Paper fish are glued into the beard.*

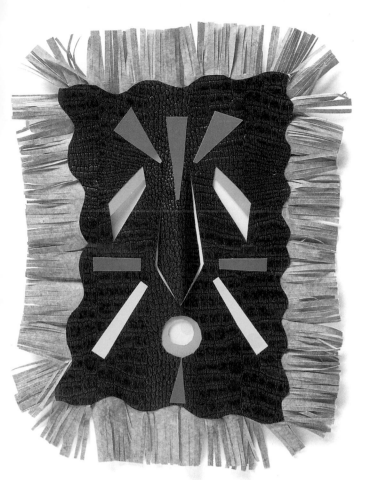

▲ *For African dance masks, cut out different shapes like these.*

▲ *For a traditional ancient Greek theater mask, cut out a shape with pointed ends and a pointed chin.*

## PAPER PLATE PIG

Make this cheeky pig, then adapt the same method to make a whole farmyard of animals.

### WHAT YOU NEED

Plain white paper plate, pink paint
Glue and glue brush
Cardboard cup, cut from an egg box
Scissors and pencil, elastic, and hole punch

**I** *Cut out eye holes and a nose hole in the right place — it's a good idea to make a scrap version first to get the positions right.*

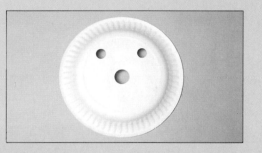

**2** *Make two holes in the end of the cardboard egg cup. Then glue it onto the mask over the nose hole, and paint the whole mask pink. Stick on pink piggy ears and attach elastic to each side.*

247

# Decorating paper

COLLECT A GOOD RANGE OF different kinds and sizes of paper. Ask people for a few sheets of writing paper, for example, and save clean wrapping paper that has come round goods or presents. There are lots of things you can do to decorate ordinary paper and make it look interesting, individual, and attractive.

## PAPER AGING

Antique paper is often stiff and browny-yellow, and is great for making messages and maps look old and valuable. You can fake it with teabags!

▲ *Draw a "treasure map" on the paper, using crayons in muted colours, such as brown and gray.*

1 *Put the teabag in the tray and pour hot water onto it. Stir the teabag round to make the water go brown. The stronger the color, the darker your paper will be.*

2 *Tear round the edges of the paper to make them rough. Lay the paper in the tea-water for a minute or two, until it gets stained with color.*

Torn edges stain darker, which helps the paper look authentic

3 *Slide the paper out of the tray and hold it up for a moment to get rid of drips. Put newspaper on a flat surface, then lay the paper on it. Tape round the edges to keep the paper smooth and flat while it dries.*

▲ *Make a "proclamation" by rolling the paper up and tying it with ribbon in a bow. When you are ready to read the proclamation pull the bow.*

## MARBLING THE EASY WAY

Marbled paper is great fun to make, and can be used instead of plain paper for lots of the projects in this book. You can buy special marbling tools and paints in craft shops, but try this easy method first to get quick results.

### WHAT YOU NEED

Oil paints thinned with white spirit, vinegar
Rubber gloves, apron and shallow baking tray
Thick cartridge paper that will fit into the baking tray
Newspaper, cocktail sticks
Paintbrushes, masking tape
Flat surface such as a wooden board

**1** Fill the tray almost to the top with water. Mix in a big splash of vinegar. Dribble up to four colors on the water. Swirl them round with a cocktail stick, or mix them by blowing gently on the surface through a straw. Drop on some extra blobs with a brush.

**2** Gently lay the paper face-down on the surface of the water. Because the paints are thinned down, they float on top of the water. Tap over the paper very gently with your finger to get rid of any air bubbles trapped beneath it.

**3** After a few moments, lift the paper up with both hands, holding each end and pulling it straight upwards. Hold it above the tray for a moment to let the excess water drain off.

**4** Lay the marbled paper, colored-side up, on top of newspaper or scrap paper laid on a flat surface. Put wet masking tape round the edges of the marbled paper to keep it smooth and flat as it dries.

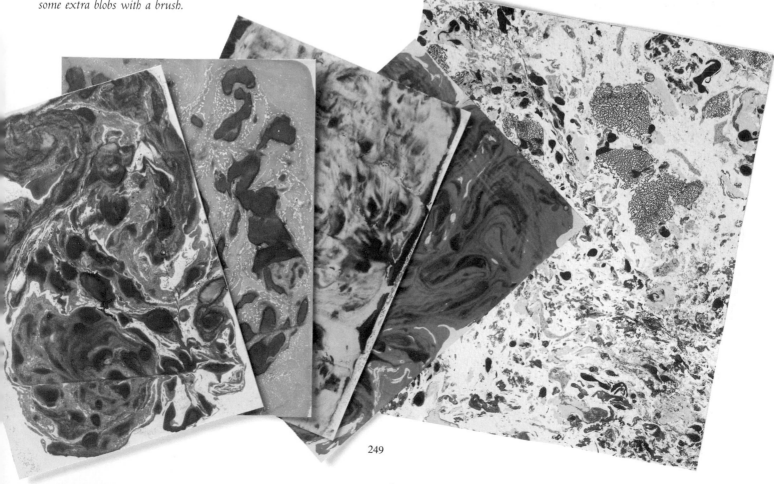

249

# Special stitching

WHAT YOU NEED
......................................................
Strong darning needle
Thread, knotted at one end
Thick paper, glue and glue brush
Backing paper
Thin drawing paper, pencil, and sticky
tape (optional)

IF YOU LIKE SEWING, YOU CAN DO IT ON more than just fabric. Try decorating paper with your needle and thread. Choose stiff paper or thin card, and use embroidery threads in different colors. You could use the ideas shown here to decorate many of the objects you have made from this book.

Sew a picture onto a gift card.

Thread beads onto the stitches you make

Decorate card edges with overstitching

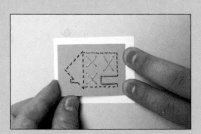

1 Tape some drawing paper on top of the thick paper, draw a design on the drawing paper, and sew through it to the paper beneath. Then cut off the drawing paper and throw it away.

2 Alternatively, you can lightly draw a design directly onto the card, and cover it up by sewing over it. After you have finished sewing, anchor the end of the thread tightly at the back with a piece of sticky tape.

3 The back of your sewing is often a bit untidy! Finish off neatly by glueing another piece of paper or card onto the back.

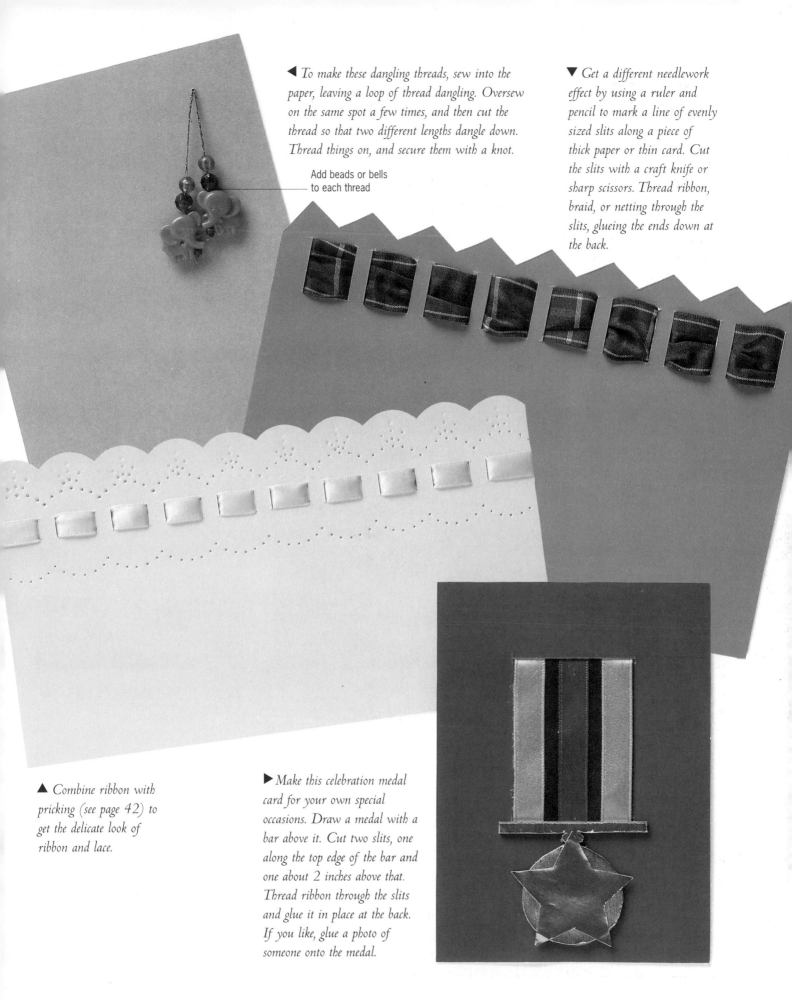

◀ *To make these dangling threads, sew into the paper, leaving a loop of thread dangling. Oversew on the same spot a few times, and then cut the thread so that two different lengths dangle down. Thread things on, and secure them with a knot.*

Add beads or bells to each thread

▼ *Get a different needlework effect by using a ruler and pencil to mark a line of evenly sized slits along a piece of thick paper or thin card. Cut the slits with a craft knife or sharp scissors. Thread ribbon, braid, or netting through the slits, glueing the ends down at the back.*

▲ *Combine ribbon with pricking (see page 42) to get the delicate look of ribbon and lace.*

▶ *Make this celebration medal card for your own special occasions. Draw a medal with a bar above it. Cut two slits, one along the top edge of the bar and one about 2 inches above that. Thread ribbon through the slits and glue it in place at the back. If you like, glue a photo of someone onto the medal.*

# Origami

ORIGAMI IS A JAPANESE WORD THAT MEANS "folding paper," an art that originated in Japan over 1,000 years ago. It can be very complicated, but the two designs shown here are simple to start with, and only need a paper square.

## SWAN

*1 Lay the paper down as a diamond-shape. Make a center fold.*

*2 Fold the left and right corners into the center.*

*3 Fold the top point down to meet the inner corners in the center.*

*4 Fold the point up 1.5 inches to make a tab.*

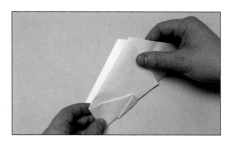

*5 Fold the model in half with the "wings" on the outside.*

*6 Pull up the head and neck so the swan stands up.*

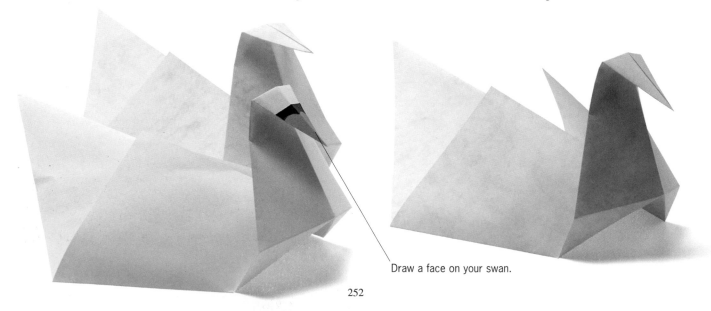

Draw a face on your swan.

252

# PAPER PLAY BALL

**1** *Start with a square of thin paper. Make valley folds down and across. Make diagonal mountain folds between the corners.*

**2** *Pull up the middle and push either side in to make a triangle.*

**3** *Working with the front layer of paper, fold the two bottom corners up to the top center.*

**4** *Turn the model over, and fold the other two corners up.*

**5** *Working with one layer, fold the left and right corners into the middle.*

**6** *Turn the model over and repeat step 5.*

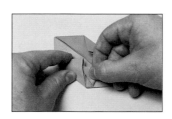

**7** *Working with one layer, fold down the two top corners and tuck them in to the tops of the triangles beneath. Turn the model over and repeat.*

**8** *Blow into the hole at the bottom end to make the ball inflate.*

Hang the ball by a loop to make a decoration

▲ *Play with the ball, or blow it along with a straw.*

▲ *Run the bottom hole of the bomb under the tap to fill it with water — then throw it quickly!*

# Origami butterfly

TRADITIONAL ORIGAMI BECAME A real art in Japan, with incredibly beautiful and complicated objects being made. What most origami objects have in common is that you can usually do something with them – either play with them, or make them move.

## BUTTERFLY

This butterfly may look difficult, but it just takes care and patience. You might like to practice first on some scrap paper until you get the folds absolutely right. Then choose some thin but strong paper for the final model.

1 Fold the square in half lengthwise and widthwise. Unfold it, and turn it over so that you can see two mountain folds.

2 Fold the paper diagonally both ways, so that you have two valley folds.

3 Pull the two points shown upward and inward to make a triangle shape.

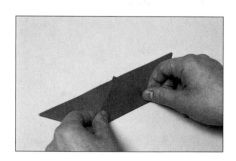

4 Fold the bottom point up to meet the top edge.

5 Fold the two bottom corners in a little, as shown in the picture.

6 Unfold these corners again, making sure that the creases hold in the paper.

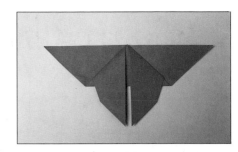

**7** *Partly unfold the top, so that you can fold the inner layers only of the bottom corners in again. The previous creases should make this easy.*

**8** *Pull down the top layer by holding the left and right corners and pulling them down to the center.*

**9** *This is the shape you should now have. You can see the butterfly shape beginning to appear.*

**10** *Pinch up the middle of the butterfly's "body."*

**11** *Fold the body out in a V-shape, on either side of the center.*

▶ *Mount your butterflies on card to make a picture, or glue one to a plant stick and push it into a plant pot for decoration.*

# Craft festivities

**M**ANY OF THE CRAFTS COVERED IN THIS BOOK can be adapted to a particular theme, such as yearly festivals in your religion. Here are some ideas for Christmas. You'll probably think of all sorts of other adaptations to the crafts shown in the book, to suit particular occasions.

### WHAT YOU NEED

Medium-weight shiny, colored paper

Scissors

Cotton thread

Glue

## BOWS AND BELLS

Pleated bows and bells made out of pretty paper can be used to decorate presents or hung up for display.

*1 To make a bell, cut a circle of paper, then mark a line into the middle from the edge, and cut along it.*

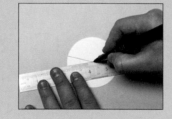

*2 Pleat around the middle, and then glue the edges together with thread running down through the middle. Knot the thread inside the bell to keep it in place.*

*1 For a bow, cut a rectangle of paper. A wide rectangle will make a "bunchy" bow; a longer rectangle will give you a longer bow.*

*2 Make narrow pleats along the long edge. Pinch the pleats together and tie thread tightly round the middle. Then fan out the pleats on either side.*

Hang up bows and bells by loops of thread

▶ *If your festival is Christmas, add shiny gold and silver bells to your Christmas tree.*

▶ *Many of the projects for party decorations can also be used for festivities, like this banner chain.*

◀ *Why not make special gift tags for your presents? You could make them match your other decorations or the wrapping paper you have made.*

▶ *Use the method shown on page 19 to make a festive gift frame for a photograph, a picture, or a piece of your own art.*

257

# Papermaking

Y OU CAN RECYCLE OLD SCRAP PAPER AND card to make your very own new paper. It's great fun to try, and you can add flat objects such as pictures or leaves to the recycled paper to make it more unusual.

## WHICH PAPER?

The paper scraps you use will determine the color and texture of the finished new paper sheet. Use writing paper or typing paper, tissue, and card. Don't use newspaper (it goes brown), or paper with a shiny coating on.

## MOLD AND DECKLE

To make paper you need a mold and a deckle. The mold is a wooden frame with netting stretched over it. The deckle is a second wooden frame without the netting. The mold catches the pulp and the deckle holds it in place. You can buy a mold from a craft shop, but it isn't difficult to make your own.

1 *Cut a piece of netting about 2 inches bigger than the picture frame all round.*

2 *Stretch the netting over the frame, and secure it all round the edges with drawing pins, pulling it tight and even. Here you can see the covered mold and the uncovered deckle.*

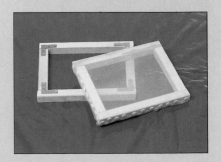

Making paper can be pretty messy, so make sure that all your work surfaces are well protected, and that you wear an apron. Try in small quantities first, until you get good at it.

1 *Soak the paper pieces in water for about an hour to soften them. Strain off the excess water. Fill the blender three-quarters full of water and add 10–15 wet paper pieces per pint. Switch on and blend until the pulp is smooth and creamy – about 30 seconds. Make six loads and pour them into the plastic bowl.*

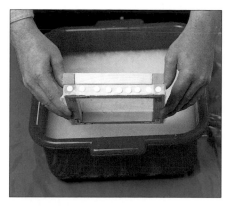

2 *Stir the pulp so that all the fibers don't sink to the bottom. Hold the mold firmly with the deckle aligned on top of it (if you are using one), and the netting in between. Stand them up at the back of the bowl with the deckle toward you.*

3 *Gently slide the mold and deckle down into the bowl toward you, until they are lying flat under the liquid pulp.*

## WRITE ON!

If you want to be able to write on your paper, you need to add "size" to the soggy paper pulp in the bowl before you mold it. This will stop ink from soaking into the paper surface when you write on the finished paper. Add two teaspoons of cold water starch to the bowl, and stir it in to the pulp.

4 *After a few moments, pull the mold and deckle straight up out of the water. The pulp will lie evenly on top of the netting. Shake it gently from side to side, and then back and forth, to spread the paper fibers.*

5 *Carefully lift the deckle away, taking care not to drag it over the pulp. Turn to the next page to see how you get the paper out of the mold and dry it.*

# Finishing paper

THE BEST WAY OF GETTING THE WET PAPER PULP out of the frame is by a process called couching (pronounced "kootching.") Although it can be the most tricky part of papermaking, it is essential if the sheet is to end up flat. The trick to successful couching and drying is simply not to rush!

### WHAT YOU NEED

Paper pulp spread evenly
on mold
Plenty of clean, absorbent cloths
Heavy books and a board
Newspaper

## COUCHING

Couching is the trick of squeezing enough water out of the wet paper pulp to allow it to fall easily out of the mold. Be patient, though — you will find that the wet paper sticks to the mold and will tear easily if not handled carefully.

*1 Lay out two dry absorbent cloths on the covered work surface. Lay the mold on top and cover with two more cloths. Pat the sandwich gently until the blotters are wet. Replace with dry blotters.*

*2 Continue doing this until the paper begins to come away from the mold when a corner is gently pulled. When it is ready, lay the mold on a new dry cloth, press down firmly and then ease the mold away, leaving the pulp behind.*

## DRYING

Don't be tempted to hurry this process up by applying heat, because that would make the paper very bumpy and uneven.

*1 Lay more dry cloths on top of the new paper, then place it between the middle pages of a newspaper. Put a board on top and weight it down with something heavy. Leave to dry. After a few hours, remove the outer layer of cloths from the newspaper and replace with fresh dry cloths and more newspaper.*

*2 Weight them with books as before, and leave to dry again. Repeat this process every six hours or so until the paper is completely dry. Then open the cloths and slip a palette knife (or an ordinary knife) under the edge of the paper all round.*

## ADDING THE FINISHING TOUCH

Once you have begun papermaking you will be able to experiment in lots of different ways. You could add texture to a sheet by drying it under a knobbly cloth. You might like to make extra-thick fibrous paper, or fine, thin sheets. And you can press fine, textured things like leaves into the paper while it dries.

▶ *Some hand-made papers are so beautiful, they become works of art all on their own, so frame them!*

**3** *Holding one edge, peel off the cloth. Be careful not to bend the paper, which might damage it.*

**4** *The paper is now finished! You can put more than one sheet of pulp under the same board, as long as you put plenty of kitchen cloths and newspaper in between each sheet.*

▶ *Mount hand-made paper on card to make your own stationery.*

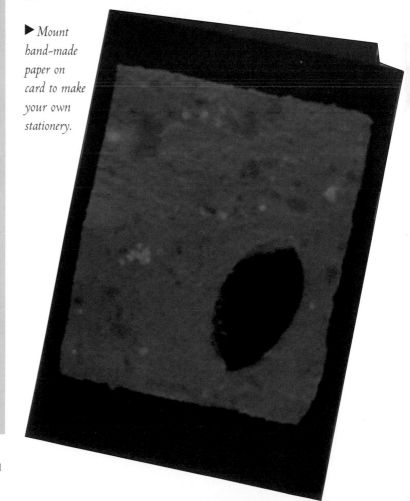

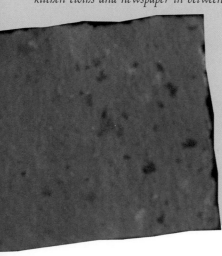

◀ *Finished pieces of homemade paper have a wonderful texture. The uneven edges just add to the effect.*